8 STEPS *to*
Energize
YOUR FAITH

Other Books by Joe Paprocki

8 STEPS *to* *Energize* YOUR FAITH

JOE PAPROCKI, DMin

LOYOLA PRESS.
A JESUIT MINISTRY
Chicago

LOYOLA PRESS.
A JESUIT MINISTRY

www.loyolapress.com

Copyright © 2022 Joe Paprocki
All rights reserved.

Scripture quotations taken from The Holy Bible, New International Version® NIV®
Copyright© 1973, 1978, 1984, 2011 by Biblica, Inc. Used with permission. All rights reserved
worldwide.

Cover art credit: Jose A. Bernat Bacete/Moment/Getty Images
Back cover author photo, supplied by author.

ISBN: 978-0-8294-5449-9
Library of Congress Control Number: 2022945486

Printed in the United States of America.
22 23 24 25 26 27 28 29 30 31 Versa 10 9 8 7 6 5 4 3 2 1

To Maureen Kuhn, my friend and spiritual director, for listening to my "scoops" every month for nearly twenty years and for reminding me that I am God's "precious one."

Contents

Acknowledgments

I would like to express my deepest gratitude to the following people: Carrie Freyer for two decades of looking out for me; Julianne Stanz, Fr. Frank DeSiano, CSP, Todd Flowerday, and Dave Gruber for reviewing my manuscript and offering valuable feedback, suggestions, and insights for improvement; Gary Jansen for pushing me to sharpen my focus and write with a sense of urgency; Vinita Hampton Wright and Mary Collins for superb editing; Joe and Maryann Sodini for a friendship that nourishes my soul; and my wife Jo, for filling me and my life with a love that is infused with divine energy.

I Wanna Live Again!

The glory of God is a man [or woman] fully alive.

—St. Irenaeus

An Angelic Intervention

After suffering serious financial setbacks, George Bailey (*It's a Wonderful Life*) comes to the realization that he is worth more dead than alive (life insurance). Standing on a bridge over turbulent waters, George is prepared to jump in and end it all. Instead, his angel, Clarence, intervenes and dives in first, thus prompting George to save him instead of taking his own life. Clarence goes on to show George just what a wonderful life he really has, which brings George to the point of begging, "I wanna live again!"

Like George Bailey, the prophet Elijah had a wake-up call. He concluded that, despite all the powerful works God had accomplished through him, he (Elijah) was a failure whose only reward was a bounty on his head and a life as an outcast, on the run from his enemies. He decided that he wanted to go to sleep under a broom tree and never wake up again. That is, until an angel intervened, tapping him and saying, "Get up and eat." Elijah got up, had some bread and something to drink, and went right back to sleep. So, his angel had to work overtime and rouse him a second time, saying, "Get up and eat,

xii 8 Steps to Energize Your Faith

for the journey is too much for you." This time, Elijah got up, ate and drank, and found the strength to travel forty days and forty nights until he reached Horeb, the mountain of God (1 Kings 19:3–9).

Both George Bailey and the prophet Elijah were in such despair that they lost their will to live, and both regained their desire to live again because of the intervention of an angel.

"I Wanna Live Again!"

The truth is, sometimes life is too much for us, just as it was for George and Elijah. And, like them, we sometimes feel as though we are burned out and don't have the wherewithal to keep going. In such cases, we need an angel to intervene; in other words, if we hope to get up and be spiritually reawakened, we need help from beyond ourselves or what we call a "divine intervention." The presence of an angel in each story signals that, when confronted with the meaning of life, we enter the spiritual realm. Like Clarence, Elijah's unnamed angel intervened to prompt Elijah to "get up" and to want to live again.

Lord knows we continue to endure turbulent times the likes of which few of us have experienced before. Our spiritual lives have been taking a beating in recent times (in our civil communities as well as in our parish/church communities), as we have attempted to navigate unprecedented experiences of a pandemic, racial strife, economic uncertainty, political divisions and acrimonious elections, rampant incivility on social media, and ideological polarization, to name a few. As a result, many of us now find that, like George Bailey and Elijah, we are losing our zest for life. This spiritual lethargy manifests itself in a variety of ways, including a tendency to withdraw, joyless recreation, feelings of despair, a sense of cynicism and negativity, spiritual disconnection, doubt, feelings of being overwhelmed, emotional and physical fatigue, and an increasing desire to "anesthetize" through overindulgence in various pleasures.

While we all experience some of the above from time to time, it is spiritually unhealthy when these feelings become chronic and our spirit is no longer able to "get up." It is when we reach that point that we are in desperate need of an angel: an intervention from God. Luckily for us, *intervening* is what God does best; it is God's "MO" to insert himself into the lives of his people. Such interventions are typically not as dramatic as George Bailey's or Elijah's, and our angel often turns out to be a friend, coworker, neighbor, or stranger in the most unlikely time or place. The good news is that, through the Holy Spirit, we have access to divine energy—not just human energy that we try to generate ourselves but God's own life!

Claiming Your Inheritance

Imagine that, after a long period of being down on your luck financially, you discover that you are the sole heir of an insanely wealthy relative who is the owner of a wildly successful corporation that has borne the family's good name for generations. Now that this relative has decided to retire, she has intervened in your life and announced that you will now take over control of the corporation and share in its abundance. There's only one stipulation: you must agree to continue upholding the company's long-standing credo, which she insists has been the key to its success. You would no doubt "do your homework" to learn your relative's philosophy and values embodied in that credo so that you could put them into practice. You would strive to live up to the family's name and emulate your relative's way of proceeding to ensure continued success for yourself and for the company. In other words, you would want this relative to reveal her mind and heart to you so that you could, in turn, embody those same values, beliefs, and principles in your role as successor.

The above scenario is an apt metaphor for how God intervenes in our lives and prompts us to "get up," reawaken our faith, and tap into divine energy. The key to this transformation comes from beyond ourselves, and we can do nothing to earn it; however, we must do some serious work to hold up our end of the bargain.

The Good News of Jesus Christ is that we are heirs to the abundant riches (graces) of God's kingdom and that we are called to begin sharing in this inheritance NOW. This is what St. Paul tells us in his letter to the Romans when he says that "we are God's children. Now if we are children, then we are heirs—heirs of God and co-heirs with Christ" (Romans 8:16–17) and again in the letter to the Ephesians when he says that we are sealed with the Holy Spirit, "guaranteeing our inheritance" (Ephesians 1:14). We are literally called to start a new life filled with an embarrassment of riches. This is the essence of discipleship: to live as an heir of God's kingdom and to invite others to share in its abundant riches.

We Have Some Work to Do

This new life, which is freely given to us, also calls us to respond in a particular manner. If we want to keep this inheritance—if we want to tap into divine energy—we have some work to do. We are called to emulate the One who bestows this gift upon us. And to emulate God, in whose image and likeness we are made, we need to ask God to reveal his heart and mind to us. Luckily, God has already done so; we see this so clearly throughout sacred Scripture and through the work of the Holy Spirit. Scripture is not so much about following rules as it is about imitating someone, namely, our Creator. This imitation of the Divine is the key to reawakening our faith and tapping into divine energy so that we can become more fully human.

This book explores the ways you can see God's "intervention" in your life, enabling it to be infused with divine energy that will make you want to get up and live again! You can do this by, first, recognizing that you are a child of God and an heir to God's abundant graces and, second, freely responding with a commitment to emulate God's "way of proceeding" as revealed in Scripture, so that you might flourish in this endeavor. In doing so, you will be able to venture further into the reawakening of your faith, which opens a path to a new or deeper relationship with God and others. In this book, we will focus on eight of these divine attributes.

Divine Attributes (God's Way of Proceeding)	What We Must Do to Emulate God
God is a creator: God's first act is to create all of reality.	Create something.
God delights in his creation: God states that everything he made is "good."	Delight in nature and all of creation.
God appreciates simplicity: God asks us to unclutter our lives and get rid of anything that makes it hard to encounter him.	Simplify your life.
God is relational: God *is* community (Father, Son, and Holy Spirit).	Build and celebrate relationships.
God is compassionate: God's primary characteristic is compassion for those who are suffering or vulnerable.	Show compassion.
God fixes things: God seeks to mend, heal, and rescue.	Make repairs.
God is generous and selfless: God's love is expressed most powerfully in Jesus, selflessly laying down his life for us.	Share generously and selflessly.
God is—he just IS!	Be still.

By engaging in the above actions, we emulate God and act as his true heirs (disciples), which enables us to enjoy the fullness of his inheritance and tap into divine energy. You'll notice that the actions I describe are not very "churchy." It is unfortunate that the notion of living a spiritual life is so often measured solely by the amount of time one spends in church or in performing pious religious practices, worthy as these practices are. After all, spending time in church doesn't make you a Christian ("holy") any more than spending time in a garage makes you a car. While I make a case for participation in the life of the Church as part of a healthy spirituality, my main focus is to illustrate how a healthy spiritual life must be cultivated and practiced in ordinary daily living, because even weekly churchgoers spend 167 of 168 hours per week in the details of everyday life.

To truly embrace the potential of divine energy to which we are heirs, we must break down the compartmentalization of faith that has led to an unfortunate and artificial separation between the sacred and the so-called "secular" and, instead, recognize the presence of God in all things, in all people, and in all of creation. It is in our daily living that we need to focus our attention; it is in daily living that the energy and direction of God need to take hold. Tapping into this divine energy gives us the ability to integrate all our life through a new vision and allows us to reflect God's life more fully.

Now Is the Time

When it comes to "getting up," renewing our spiritual life, and tapping into divine energy, we cannot simply wait for the negative circumstances around us to change so that they bother us less. That rarely happens. Rather, we must change our hearts and minds so that we more closely emulate God, who wants us to begin enjoying our inheritance now.

Don't be lulled into thinking that God's plan is for us to grit our teeth and endure this messy world to earn some kind of eternal "reward" in the afterlife. Although this sentiment too often pervades Christian thinking (as revealed by this verse of the evangelical spiritual "I'll Fly Away": "Just a few more weary days and then, I'll fly away; to a land where joy shall never end, I'll fly away"), you will not find such sentiment in the Bible! Instead, we are called to embrace the words of St. Paul, who recognized that we don't have to wait to begin enjoying our inheritance: "Now is the time of God's favor, now is the day of salvation" (2 Corinthians 6:2). With the help of the Holy Spirit, let's get up and start living—tapping into divine energy—NOW!

Chapter 1

Create Something

You can't use up creativity. The more you use, the more you have.

—Maya Angelou

In the Beginning

Hopefully, you know by now that the Bible story of God creating the world in six days and resting on the seventh (Genesis 1:1—2:3) is not meant to be taken literally. Science—especially astronomy and geology—has provided us with a scientific understanding of creation, including the Big Bang (first proposed by Jesuit Fr. George Lemaître, an astronomer, mathematician, and physicist) and evolution (which included early contributions by Jesuit-educated French scientist Jean-Baptiste Lamarck and Augustinian monk Gregor Mendel). By no means, however, does that mean we can dismiss the biblical account of creation! In fact, it compels us to embrace that account with greater reverence because we now know that it was and is intended not to convey facts but rather to reveal spiritual truth.

We can see God's creativity in the way God inspires the first stories of the Bible. We know these stories are imaginative ways to convey the deepest truths of human existence and experience, not the least of which include insights into where we came from and why we exist. God uses the imaginations of Hebrew people to call us to see something that eyes and observation alone cannot see: everything springs from God's creative and life-giving love. With that in mind, we come to the main point of this chapter: one of the first spiritual truths revealed about God in Scripture is that *God is very creative,* and we can tap into divine energy by practicing creativity.

Who do you know who is very creative? In what way(s) does he or she show that creativity?

_____

_____

_____

God Is Soooo Creative

To *create* is to bring something into existence through imaginative skill. In Scripture, the very first thing that God does is imagine the cosmos into existence. In fact, I have gone as far as to say (in my book *Under the Influence of Jesus*) that God does primarily two things: God creates and God restores. And God does both things really well! Scripture begins with God creating something out of nothing, a power that magicians have long attempted to persuade audiences they possess. The Genesis account of creation tells us that God brings all of reality into existence simply by speaking—that is, by willing it to be. The account tells us that this is done out of love and in an orderly (not chaotic) fashion and that God sees all of creation as good.

The creation story in the first chapter of Genesis portrays God as an artist who adds light, darkness, colors, shapes, textures, and ultimately beings to the cosmic canvas, while the second creation story in the second chapter of Genesis portrays God as the potter who artistically forms the first humans. For those who enjoy doing craft activities, it's nice to know that God's first act was just that: a cosmic craft activity! Creativity is nothing less than a divine attribute. As people made in the image and likeness of God, we resemble God when we express ourselves creatively, when we bring something into existence through imaginative skill. Suffice it to say, engaging in some type of creative experience is a healthy way to tap into divine energy and to imitate our Creator, who proudly boasts, "I am making everything new!" (Revelation 21:5).

> **Creativity expresses itself in many ways: you don't have to be an artist to be creative. On a scale of 1–10 (1 = not very creative; 10 = extremely creative), how would you rate yourself? Explain why.**
>
> _____
>
> _____
>
> _____

What Is Creativity?

Creativity is driven by our desire to make a physical expression of an idea, an impulse, a dream, a thought, or an intuition. Creativity begins in the imagination, which means that it begins in the nonphysical world, what many would call the "spiritual" world. The imagination enables us to not only see reality but also see meaning hidden in the depths of that reality; in other words, it enables us to envision an alternate reality or to think about the world in different ways. Thus, creativity cultivates "spirituality," or a relationship and encounter with mystery. Likewise, authentic spirituality—our hunger for meaning beyond that which meets the eye—cultivates creativity. We can say that creativity enriches our souls and that by engaging in creative activities, we can build our spiritual "intelligence." In her article "The Relationship Between Spirituality and Artistic Expression: Cultivating the Capacity for Imagining" (*Spirituality in Higher Education,* ucla.edu), artist, spiritual director, and theologian Christine Valters Paintner, PhD, explains that such spiritual intelligence can lead to transformation because it provides us with "a set of values to live by, a sense of direction, and a basis for hope."

With the discovery of etchings on cave walls dating back tens of thousands of years, archeology continues to reveal that creativity is a primal human instinct. Early childhood experts tell us that creativity begins very early and reaches its peak for many children before the age of six. We human beings are born with a drive to explore the world around us. We are naturally curious and naturally creative. Before beginning to use words, children rely on symbols and images to express themselves and to create things. We are created to be creative! This creativity can often be diminished by the pressures of a culture that emphasizes and measures success by achievement. We live in a society that cherishes "left-brain" thinking and too often downplays the importance of creativity (a right-brain activity) in favor of test scores. But we must never forget that "success"—however that is defined—relies on creativity. Creativity is essential for success and holds the power to unlock hearts and connect us with that which cannot be measured empirically.

When we engage in creative activities, time seems to disappear. We can lose ourselves and be swept away into something beyond ourselves and, in doing so, we experience joy, freedom, renewal, and energy. Engaging in creative activity usually results in a feeling of being more centered. In essence, when we create something, that which we have created, re-creates us. As Pope John Paul II writes in his *Letter to Artists* (1999), "Not all are called to be artists in the specific sense of the term. Yet, as Genesis has it, all men and women are entrusted with the task of crafting their own life: in a certain sense, they are to make of it a work of art, a masterpiece."

When, where, and how do you feel you are at your most creative?

_____

_____

_____

What's Your Creative Outlet?

Creativity is not reserved for artists, musicians, writers, and other obvious creatives. While it's true that many people are gifted with so much creativity that they can make a living from it, that does not mean that the rest of us do not have creativity. Some people's careers lend themselves to creativity:

interior designers	graphic designers
hairdressers	marketers
architects	fashion designers
teachers	florists
chefs	event planners

website designers   inventors
editors   leaders and problem solvers
photographers   other _____
property stagers

. . . .just to name a few.

In addition to careers as a creative outlet, we also can engage in hobbies that provide opportunities to express ourselves creatively:

cooking, beer brewing, wine   model building
  making   car restoration
gardening   antique restoration
singing, playing an instrument,   historical reenactment
  composing music   performing magic, clowning
drawing, painting, sculpting   photography, videography,
dancing, acting   filmmaking
writing, blogging   scrapbooking, making cards, let-
crafts, woodworking, metal   ter writing, journaling/bullet
  working   journaling
sewing, needlework, quilting,   other _____
  cross-stitching, leather working,
  knitting

While there are many other hobbies that are engaging and healthy, the ones listed above are particularly good for encouraging creativity. By engaging in creative activities, we open ourselves up to the Divine—to the Creator of the Universe—in whose image and likeness we have been made. As Australian artist and creativity coach Jassy Watson explains in a blog post:

> It is standing before the canvas, a portal of possibility, that I can completely surrender, invite, and allow my spirit to awaken and divine spirit to flow through me. I merely become a vessel. Is it my hand painting this picture? I blur my vision and through squinted

eyes I paint and seek, and for a moment, just out of the corner of my eye, I catch a glimpse of a parallel dimension. Learning to open up and allow this essence to flow with complete trust, to communicate, express and bring into form my deepest held beliefs, ideas, and visions, is a divine gift, and one that requires daily practice and nurturance. Not only because art making is my job and purpose, but because it is my spiritual practice. ("Creativity as Spirituality," July 9, 2014)

> **How are you able to express or practice creativity at work or in some other venue in daily living? What hobby allows you to express yourself creatively?**
>
> _____
>
> _____
>
> _____

Because only God can literally create something out of nothing, every time we create something, we put ourselves in touch with God because we must rely on what God has already created. The following joke is a good illustration of what I'm talking about:

One day the scientists decided that humanity no longer needed God, so one of them went to God, bearing the news. "God," he said, "we don't need you anymore. We can create things without your help. We can clone people on our own. So why don't you just get lost?" God was patient and kind. "Very well," He replied. "If that is how you feel, let's resolve this with a contest. Let us see who can make a human being." "Sure," said the scientist, "that's fine with me." "But there is one condition," said God. "We will do this just the way it was done the first time when I created Adam." "Sure, no problem," said the scientist. He bent down to grab a handful of dirt. "No, no, no," said God. "You go make your own dirt."

What this means is, our creativity is a response to, a cooperation with, and an expression of God's creativity, which precedes us. No matter what we create, the ingredients come from God. The ultimate example of this is, of course, procreation, the making of new life. When spouses conceive new life through the conjugal act, they participate in God's creative power—which is precisely why the conjugal act is traditionally revered as sacred: it is a participation in God's holy creativity. Although we cannot create the way God does, our creativity responds to and participates in God's creativity, bringing God's creation to greater perfection.

How can/does participating in creative activities open you to the Divine?

_____

_____

_____

Creativity and Healing

In recent times, some have come to view creativity as much more than a frivolous hobby, recognizing it as a form of healing therapy for people coping with the burdens of a variety of debilitating conditions, including the often-invisible wounds of post-traumatic stress disorder (PTSD). Creativity enables individuals to overcome a sense of helplessness and hopelessness that conditions such as PTSD create, thus enabling them to process traumatic events in a helpful way. Creative therapies enable individuals to express themselves nonverbally, which reduces the anxiety of language-based approaches. Such approaches have been shown to reduce blood pressure, boost the immune system, promote relaxation, reduce pain, and promote general quality of life (The Foundation for Art & Healing/The Unlonely Project). According to art therapist Gretchen Miller, "Art expression is a powerful way to safely contain and create separation from the terrifying experience of trauma" and "safely gives voice to and makes a survivor's experience of emotions, thoughts, and memories visible when words are insufficient" (from "The Value of Art Expression in Trauma-Informed Work").

While many of us are not bearing such dramatic burdens, we all can benefit from the healing effects of creativity that bring us into the divine life, a life characterized by creating and restoring.

Whatever we create, the very act of creativity opens us up to the flow of divine life, which is a healing force. To be creative is to create a new moment, a new direction, and a new perspective. Research reveals that engaging in creative activity improves positive emotions and reduces feelings of depression and anxiety. Creativity reduces isolation since we are driven to share that which we create with others. It also helps us to express our emotions in ways that may or may not involve words. It is this outward movement of creativity that holds the potential for healing.

> **Where in your life do you need healing? How can creativity and creative expression be a source of healing for you?**
>
> _____
>
> _____
>
> _____

Creativity as Proactivity

The story of creation in the book of Genesis is a story of proactivity: God initiates creation and rests on the seventh day only after his creative work is accomplished. This tells us that if we are to resemble God and be spiritually healthy, it behooves us to be proactive in our creative efforts as opposed to falling into a passive mode, which can lead to lethargy or sloth.

Dr. Martin Luther King Jr. once said, "As my sufferings mounted, I soon realized that there were two ways in which I could respond to my situation—either to react with bitterness or seek to transform the suffering into a creative force. I decided to follow the latter course." This creative force is always at our fingertips; however, we often lack the proactivity to seize the moment.

In his famous book *The 7 Habits of Highly Effective People*, Stephen Covey identifies the first habit as *being proactive*. Proactivity and creativity go hand in hand. The proactive person creates his or her own possibilities and events instead of waiting for opportunities or reacting to events.

In what situations do you find yourself most proactive? In which situations do you feel you can and should be more proactive?

_____

_____

_____

Creativity and Visualization

Our minds are constantly creating, beginning with our dreams while we sleep and continuing through the moment we awaken and begin to visualize what we will eat, what we will wear, what we will do at work, what we will say in a given situation, and so on. To visualize is to create a mental picture of your desired outcomes: if I want to look professional today, I picture myself in a suit and tie and then proceed to create that look. Visualization is a technique that many people follow to "mentally rehearse" their day in hopes of creating a day that matches their hopes, dreams, and desires. Visualizing is a step toward creating a new reality.

Saint Ignatius of Loyola encouraged such visualization as part of prayer and the life of discipleship. This practice is known as contemplation and is a significant feature of his *Spiritual Exercises*. Saint Ignatius believed that God speaks to us through our imaginations as well as through our thoughts and memories. In particular, Ignatius encourages retreatants to visualize the Gospel stories, paying attention to details including what we see, hear, taste, smell, and feel. In this creative moment, we encounter the Lord, who is present to us and communicating with us.

In his book *Reimagining the Ignatian Examen*, Mark E. Thibodeaux, SJ, explains that

> Ignatius was a master daydreamer. He could do it for hours on end. It was through daydreaming that Ignatius learned to determine God's will for his life. He learned that God communicated God's will through great desires for faith, hope, and love that welled up inside his heart and soul. By daydreaming in the context of prayer, Ignatius was able to allow those great desires to surface. Doing so would not only reveal God's will but also would fire him up to have the necessary passion to perform these great works.

Through this creative technique, we get to know Jesus better and in a different manner than we do solely through studying theology because this technique aims for the heart rather than just the head. Through the gift of creativity and the ability to visualize, we can deepen our relationship with Jesus, picturing his face, hearing his voice, "watching" how he interacts with others, and feeling his embrace of our whole person.

How can/does visualization play a part in your daily living? How can/does visualization enhance your prayer life?

_____

_____

_____

Being Fed by the Creativity of Others

We human beings are very resourceful: since not all of us possess the most creative talents, we have found ways of benefiting from the creativity of others! We may think of this simply as "entertainment"; however, the bottom line is that we consider ourselves fed and nurtured when we watch and experience the creativity of others. It is for this reason that we attend events such as the following in which creative people perform for us:

opera	athletics/sports
ballet	magic act
dance recital/performance	art exhibit
theater (plays, musicals,	craft fair
stage shows)	poetry reading
cinema	comedy
music (bands, singers, rappers,	
orchestra, etc.)	

. . . .to name a few. Our souls recognize creativity whether it is being exercised by ourselves or by someone else. Simply by observing creative people in action, we can be swept up in emotion. So, if you are not feeling particularly creative yourself, don't hesitate to feed off the creativity of others! We benefit by being exposed to the creativity of others because it brings us closer to the creative mind and heart of God.

What type of creativity do you most enjoy watching/observing? Why?

_____

_____

Creativity and Orderliness

Creative expression most often involves some sense of order. Creative performers typically begin with an agreed-upon structure. Consider jazz musicians who, even when improvising, are typically following some sort of pattern. This echoes another aspect of God's creativity: it is orderly. The creation story of Genesis tells us that God created order out of chaos and that it followed a pattern. Over the course of six days,

1. God speaks.
2. God's command is fulfilled.
3. God declares that his creation is good.
4. Evening and morning follow.

The message of this account is that God's creativity is not haphazard but is characterized by orderliness. What does this mean for us? It means that bringing order out of chaos is Godlike! Creating or restoring order at home, in your garage, in your workshop, in your she-shed, in your yard, in your neighborhood, or at work is imitating a divine act. So, if you want to feel a bit more Godlike, take a few moments to put some things in order, since that, in and of itself, is a creative act. And this goes beyond tidying up; you can order your life by setting out clear priorities and goals that guide your thinking and acting.

What area of your life is experiencing chaos and can benefit from some orderliness?

_____

_____

The Apple Didn't Fall Far

It is not uncommon for children of superstars to become superstars in their own right. Actor Laura Dern is the daughter of actor Bruce Dern. Actor John David Washington is the son of actor Denzel Washington. In the world of sports, Bobby Hull and his son Brett Hull are both members of the Hockey Hall of Fame. Ken Griffey Sr. and Gordie Howe each had the unique experience of playing professionally with their superstar sons (Ken Griffey Jr. and Mark and Marty Howe). And, of course, the Manning family produced three superstar quarterbacks: Archie and his sons Payton and Eli. You get the idea. In each case, "the apple did not fall far from the tree," with the children inheriting talents, skills, and characteristics of their famous and talented parents.

As children of God, we have inherited many of God's traits and characteristics. God's creativity is in our DNA. We can either squander this inheritance or invite the Holy Spirit to help us put it to good use so that when we exercise our creativity, we will move one step closer to resembling the Creator of the Universe and share in divine energy.

When was a time that you felt a surge of creativity flowing through you? Describe the experience.

_____

_____

_____

In Summary . . .

God's first act was to create all of reality. We can participate in the divine life and tap into divine energy by expressing ourselves creatively and engaging in (or observing) creative activities. Creativity is embedded in our human DNA. By engaging in creative activity, we embrace the divine attribute that we inherited as children of God, and we become more fully human.

Scripture Passages That Reveal/ Emphasize God's Creativity

In the beginning God created the heavens and the earth. Now the earth was formless and empty, darkness was over the surface of the deep, and the Spirit of God was hovering over the waters.
Genesis 1:1–2

By the word of the LORD were the heavens made,
their starry host by the breath of his mouth.
Psalm 33:6

Do you not know?
    Have you not heard?
The LORD is the everlasting God,
the Creator of the ends of the earth.
    He will not grow tired or weary,
and his understanding no one can fathom.
Isaiah 40:28

Therefore, if anyone is in Christ, he is a new creation; the old has gone, the new has come!
2 Corinthians 5:17

For we are God's workmanship, created in Christ Jesus to do good works, which God prepared in advance for us to do.
Ephesians 2:10

Which of the above Scripture quotes speaks to you most strongly about God's creativity? Why?

_____

_____

_____

As you reflect on this chapter, what is one shift you can make in your life to tap into the divine energy of creativity?

_____

_____

_____

Chapter 2

Delight in Nature and All of Creation

When I admire the wonders of a sunset or the beauty of the moon,
my soul expands in the worship of the creator.
—Mahatma Gandhi

God Loves to Take a Stroll

How do you think God spends his evenings? According to the book of Genesis, you can find God taking a stroll in his garden, enjoying the cool of the day (Genesis 3:8). Apparently, God takes delight in his creation and likes to stop and smell his roses. This story teaches us that after he completed his creation, God did not remove himself from it. Quite the opposite. God truly delights in creation and remains intimately involved with it, infusing creation with his presence. In our first chapter, we focused on God's creativity. In this chapter, we focus on the fact that God really loves what he created and remains present and active in our lives and in the world today.

The first story of creation in Genesis reveals that several times during his workweek, God stood back and surveyed all he had created and "saw that it was good." Indeed, God derives great satisfaction from creation—the work of his hands. And rightly so. He knocked it out of the ballpark. I mean, really, the Grand Canyon, Niagara Falls, panda bears, the rain forests of the Amazon River basin, Mount Everest, eagles, butterflies, the Great Barrier Reef, Aurora Borealis, otters, giant redwood trees, the Sahara . . . not too shabby for six days' work! What's not to like?

As people made in the image and likeness of God, we have an inherent love for God's creation. In fact, we humans were "hired" to assist God in taking care of his creation. In the second chapter of Genesis, we learn that "the LORD God took the man and put him in the Garden of Eden *to work it and take care of it*" (v. 15, italics added). We got our start working in the garden, taking care of God's creation. There is a reason that we often make plans to go on vacation in locations that put us in touch with the beauty of nature and the majesty of God's creation. We feel at home there. Unfortunately, however, people today in general take much of this beauty and majesty for granted and, in fact, have destroyed far too much of it. If we want to truly tap into divine energy, we need to make amends with Mother Nature and resolve to take better care of this amazing gift.

What are some of your favorite aspects of God's creation?

_____

_____

_____

But That Can't Be How It Happened!

It's interesting to note that the creation story mentioned above (Genesis 1–2) was authored during the time of the Babylonian exile, when the Jewish people found themselves separated from their own homeland and their own culture. To their horror, they realized that their children were being indoctrinated in Babylonian mythology, which included an epic that described creation as the result of vengeful violence between angry gods. This did not resonate with what the Jewish people believed God had revealed about himself. Their God was a merciful God, slow to anger and rich in kindness. Surely God created all of creation as an act of love, and they wanted their children to know this. Thus, the book of Genesis was born, and with it, the story of creation as an act of love resulting in beauty and goodness for humankind to enjoy.

Another interesting point about this story is that the creation of human beings is not the climax of the story. Of the six days of creation, humans are created last, and the story does not end there but climaxes with God resting on the seventh day. The message is clear: while humans have a preeminent role, we are "lumped in" with the rest of creation. We are intimately related to all of creation, not separated from it. No doubt this is why so many ancient cultures had such reverence for nature: they saw themselves as being intimately related to all of creation. Indeed, the Judeo-Christian tradition is no different, but along the way we seem to have forgotten this important fact. God, our Father, is calling his children to return to this understanding of the interconnectedness of humankind with all of creation and, if we wish to resemble God, we must embody this divine attribute and take delight in creation, striving to protect and preserve it for the amazing gift it is.

What are some of the ways you can/do work to protect, restore, and renew God's creation?

_____

_____

_____

Our Common Home

It is for this reason that in 2015, Pope Francis wrote his encyclical letter *Laudato Si'*—an "urgent challenge to protect our common home—to bring the whole human family together to seek a sustainable and integral development, for we know that things can change" (13). Pope Francis made it abundantly clear that caring for the environment is not only a constitutive part of a life of discipleship but is also a spiritual practice because, in doing so, we preserve and protect our relationship with God and others by recognizing our interconnectedness.

It should come as no surprise that a pope named Francis would write an encyclical letter about caring for God's creation; his namesake, St. Francis of Assisi, is the patron saint of animals and ecology. Today, centuries after St. Francis lived, Franciscan spirituality continues to be characterized by a love for all of creation and continues to be a powerful inspirational force in ecological movements. Franciscan spirituality is incarnational—it is very "earthy"—and centers around the belief that God loves his creation so much that he couldn't resist entering it in the flesh. It is significant to note that Franciscan philosopher and theologian John Duns Scotus insisted that God created the universe with the

Incarnation (Jesus becoming flesh) in mind: it wasn't plan B after things "went wrong." Scotus believed firmly that God intended all along to enter his creation in the flesh because he loved it so much.

Saint Francis of Assisi is known for his love of animals. It's not a sentimental love, however. Francis recognized a "kinship" with creation and saw animals and nature as fellow creatures, referring to them as "brother" and "sister" as captured in his well-known "Canticle of Brother Son and Sister Moon":

> Most High, all-powerful, all-good Lord, All praise is Yours,
> all glory, all honor and all blessings.
> To you alone, Most High, do they belong, and no mortal
> lips are worthy to pronounce Your Name.

> Praised be You my Lord with all Your creatures,
> especially Sir Brother Sun,
> Who is the day through whom You give us light.
> And he is beautiful and radiant with great splendor,
> Of You Most High, he bears the likeness.

> Praised be You, my Lord, through Sister Moon and
> the stars,
> In the heavens you have made them bright, precious
> and fair.

> Praised be You, my Lord, through Brothers Wind and Air,
> And fair and stormy, all weather's moods,
> by which You cherish all that You have made.

> Praised be You my Lord through Sister Water,
> So useful, humble, precious and pure.

> Praised be You my Lord through Brother Fire,
> through whom You light the night and he is beautiful and
> playful and robust and strong.
> Praised be You my Lord through our Sister,
> Mother Earth

who sustains and governs us,
producing varied fruits with colored flowers and herbs.
Praise be You my Lord through those who grant pardon for
     love of You and bear sickness and trial.

Blessed are those who endure in peace, By You Most High,
     they will be crowned.

Praised be You, my Lord through Sister Death,
from whom no-one living can escape. Woe to those who die
     in mortal sin! Blessed are they She finds doing
     Your Will.

No second death can do them harm. Praise and bless my
     Lord and give Him thanks,
And serve Him with great humility.

Francis's Canticle reveals a deep and profound theology and spirituality. Francis believed that every part of creation is an expression of God's generous love, and he considered creation to be the first "book of revelation" as well as a "sacrament"—a tangible expression of the intangible God. Although Francis surrendered all his material possessions, he wasn't rejecting our material life. Rather, he felt that we do not show enough respect for the material world—we do not give authentic witness to the divine attribute of caring for creation—and end up treating it superficially.

What have you learned about God through creation? What aspects or details of creation bring you the most delight?

_____

_____

A Portal to Deeper Spirituality

Francis saw the natural world as a vehicle for conversion, and because spirituality is ultimately about conversion—a deepening of our relationship with the Divine—we can experience conversion and grow in resemblance to our Creator by encountering nature and creation. This incarnational spirituality was/is not confined to the Franciscans! Jesuit poet Gerard Manley Hopkins's poem "God's Grandeur" eloquently captures and expresses this incarnational spirituality:

> The world is charged with the grandeur of God.
>   It will flame out, like shining from shook foil;
>   It gathers to a greatness, like the ooze of oil
> Crushed. Why do men then now not reck his rod?
> Generations have trod, have trod, have trod;
>   And all is seared with trade; bleared, smeared with toil;
>   And wears man's smudge and shares man's smell: the soil
> Is bare now, nor can foot feel, being shod.
>
> And for all this, nature is never spent;
>   There lives the dearest freshness deep down things;
> And though the last lights off the black West went
>   Oh, morning, at the brown brink eastward, springs—
> Because the Holy Ghost over the bent
>   World broods with warm breast and with ah!
>   bright wings.

It is no accident that most retreat centers, traditional seminaries, monasteries, hermitages, and the principal houses for religious communities are located in pastoral settings, where visitors, retreatants, and residents can walk through nature and expect to bump into God as Adam and Eve did in the garden.

It is no secret, then, that the natural world serves as a significant portal to a deeper spirituality. As always, however, the challenge is to extend our encounters with God in nature to the rest of our lives.

Saint Ignatius of Loyola referred to this as "finding God in all things," or the belief that all of reality, including our experiences, holds the opportunity to encounter the Divine. Many people find that time spent in nature can serve as the catalyst for developing and/or renewing this contemplative vision for life. In fact, while writing this book, I often find myself taking a break to step into my backyard for inspiration before continuing to the next idea, thought, or chapter. And that's precisely what I'm going to do right now. I'll see you in the next paragraph!

What are some of the ways that you allow yourself to be nourished by God's creation in your daily life?

_____

_____

_____

Jesus Had a Kinship with Creation

Jesus himself showed a great affinity for nature.

- He was born surrounded by animals.
- Upon being baptized by John in the river Jordan, he went immediately on retreat in the desert (the wilderness) for forty days.
- He often went by himself to quiet, deserted, solitary places.
- He invited his tired disciples to come with him to a quiet, deserted place to rest.

- After the Last Supper, he went out to pray in the garden.
- He enjoyed fishing with his friends.
- He delivered the Beatitudes in a sermon on a mountaintop.
- He used mud to heal the eyes of a blind man.
- He entered Jerusalem on a donkey.
- He used the following images from nature in his parables: seeds, soil, weeds, wheat, fish, yeast, trees, storms, rocks, sand, sparrows, sheep, goats, and vineyards.

And, while Jesus occasionally taught in a synagogue, someone's home, or the Temple in Jerusalem, most often his venue was the "cathedral of nature": seashores, hillsides, grassy areas, deserted areas, plains, and mountaintops.

Where is your personal "cathedral of nature" where you can invite creation to inspire you?

_____

_____

_____

Pets!

Few things connect us to nature more than having a pet! Today, more than ever, people seem to appreciate the value of having a pet of some kind, usually a dog or a cat. One experience years ago opened my eyes to the special connection people have with their pet. When I was in college, my cousins' beloved dog Barney passed away. Not long after

Barney passed, we were with our cousins and, for whatever reason, I and some of my siblings made a reference to Barney's passing. No sooner had we done this than my cousin Karen started to cry. I had never seen anyone cry over the loss of a pet, and I certainly didn't think of my cousin as the least bit eccentric. Now I realize that people truly have meaningful connections with their pets and think of them as family members.

In fact, according to Amanda Lee of the Chopra Center for Well-being, there are spiritual benefits to having pets.

- They increase our ability to enjoy the present moment.
- They enable us to feel contentment.
- They inspire us to be nonjudgmental.
- They invite us to be more adaptable to changing circumstances.
- They provide us with unconditional love.
- They provide us with devotion and loyalty.
- They inspire us to "stay" in the heart rather than in the mind.

(*7 Spiritual Lessons from Your Pet,* chopra.com; 4/12/17)

In recent years, pets have begun to play a bigger role in healing and therapy because they resonate with us in a way that humans are often incapable of. Studies show that interaction with therapy pets can increase oxytocin and dopamine (mood-boosting hormones) and decrease cortisol (a stress hormone). Studies also reveal that people with a pet recover more quickly from surgery, while elderly pet owners, on the average, live longer and healthier lives than those who don't own pets. In a sense, all pets are "therapy pets."

What experience(s) have you had with pets? How do pets help you or people you know to be more spiritual?

_____

_____

_____

The Benefits of Loving Creation

We know that it's a good thing to get outside occasionally and "get some fresh air"—it improves our physical and mental health. Researchers report that spending time in nature improves short-term memory, reduces stress, increases our ability to focus, reduces inflammation, eliminates fatigue, helps fight depression and anxiety, and lowers blood pressure. There are also some profound spiritual implications of spending more time encountering creation.

- It reminds us that we are part of something bigger than ourselves and puts things in perspective.
- It enables us to absorb the generative energy of the natural world.
- It reminds us to just be.
- It reminds us of our interconnectedness to creation and to one another.
- It inspires wonder and awe, which leads to joy, gratitude, and humility.
- It reminds us of our own fragility.

- It reminds us of the healing that takes place in nature and within ourselves.
- It opens us up to mystery.
- It gives us a break from technology.

What benefits do you experience most from spending time in nature?

_____

_____

_____

How to Stop and Smell the Roses

So, how can you embrace creation? Here are just a few ways you can stop and smell the roses.

watch/listen to birds
look at stars, clouds, the moon
feel the sun on your face
watch the wind blow branches
 and leaves
go camping
go fishing
take a walk in the rain (with or
 without an umbrella)
do gardening
ride your bike
volunteer at a pet shelter
collect shells, rocks, or leaves

walk barefoot through the grass
pick up litter
take nature pictures
watch nature programs on TV
watch a sunrise/sunset
sit in your backyard or at a park
visit a forest preserve, nature preserve, or state/national park
bring some plants into
 your home
sketch nature
walk a friend's dog or volunteer
 to pet-sit

**Which of the above can you add to your repertoire of ways
to connect with nature?**

_____

_____

_____

The Sacraments—Especially the Eucharist—Are Earthy

We would be remiss not to point out that the sacraments and sacramentals of the Catholic Church are closely tied to creation. They use natural elements to signify the presence of the Divine: water, fire, oil, bread, wine, ashes, palms, beeswax, and so on. In particular, the Eucharist, which is the source and summit of the spiritual life for Catholics, uses wheat and grapes. These have been formed into bread and wine as the substances through which we consume Divinity: the Body and Blood of Jesus Christ. In fact, the prayers at the preparation of the altar point this out explicitly:

> Blessed are you, Lord God of all creation,
> for through your goodness we have received
> the bread we offer you:
> fruit of the earth and work of human hands,
> it will become for us the bread of life.

> Blessed are you, Lord God of all creation,
> for through your goodness we have received
> the wine we offer you:

fruit of the vine and work of human hands,
it will become our spiritual drink.

The God we receive in Holy Communion is indeed the God of all creation and he has chosen to come to us through the "fruit of the earth" and the "fruit of the vine." Pope Francis elaborated on this in *Laudato Si'* when he wrote:

> The Lord, in the culmination of the mystery of the Incarnation, chose to reach our intimate depths through a fragment of matter. He comes not from above, but from within, he comes that we might find him in this world of ours. In the Eucharist, fullness is already achieved; it is the living center of the universe, the over-flowing core of love and of inexhaustible life. Joined to the incarnate Son, present in the Eucharist, the whole cosmos gives thanks to God." (236)

God does indeed love his creation in that he has chosen to reveal his presence through ordinary elements of that creation. In reference to the Eucharist, Saint Augustine famously said, "See what you believe . . . become what you see." The very purpose of receiving the Eucharist is to become like Christ—to resemble God and embody the divine attributes. And now I have succeeded in doing what has never been done before: I brought the Franciscans, Jesuits, and Augustinians all together on the same page (or at least in the same chapter)!

What elements from nature most convey Jesus' divine presence to you?

_____

_____

In Summary . . .

God's presence is reflected in the natural world and in all of creation. When God created the world, he did not remove himself from it but rather remains actively involved in caring for his creation. The natural world is a vehicle for conversion—for the deepening of our spirituality. We can become more fully human and tap into divine energy by spending time in nature, savoring the experience, and caring for creation.

Scripture Passages That Reveal/ Emphasize God's Delight in Nature

God saw all that he had made, and it was very good.
Genesis 1:31

Then the man and his wife heard the sound of the LORD God as he was walking in the garden in the cool of the day.
Genesis 3:8

This is what God the LORD says—
he who created the heavens and stretched them out,
    who spread out the earth and all that comes out of it,
who gives breath to its people,
    and life to those who walk on it.
Isaiah 42:5

Look at the birds of the air; they do not sow or reap or store away in barns, and yet your heavenly Father feeds them. Are you not much more valuable than they? Who of you by worrying can add a single hour to his life? And why do you worry about clothes? See how the lilies of the field grow. They do not labor or spin. Yet I tell you that not even Solomon in all his splendor was dressed like one of these.

Matthew 6:26–29

For since the creation of the world God's invisible qualities—his eternal power and divine nature—have been clearly seen, being understood from what has been made, so that men are without excuse.

Romans 1:20

Which of the above Scripture quotes speaks to you most strongly about God's delight in nature? Why?

As you reflect on this chapter, what is one shift you can make in your life to tap into the divine energy of taking delight in nature?

_____

_____

_____

Chapter 3

Simplify Your Life

We are happy in proportion to the things we can do without.
—Henry David Thoreau

Who Does God "Hang With"?

We have looked at where God likes to hang out (in creation/nature), and what he likes to do (create and repair). But what about WHO God likes to hang with? Certainly, God loves all his children; however—and this may come as a surprise to you—Scripture shows us that God has a preference. Simply put, God likes simple folks.

While there are many instances throughout Scripture that show this preference, one of my favorites is in the Gospel of Luke, when the Gospel writer offers a very cheeky introduction to the ministry of John the Baptist. What's so cheeky about it? Well, the Gospel writer announces the names of all the "big shots" of that time—the people in whom one might think God would take an interest. However, in the end, God bypasses all of them and selects a "no name" as his number-one draft pick:

> In the fifteenth year of the reign of TIBERIUS CAESAR—when
> PONTIUS PILATE was governor of Judea, HEROD tetrarch of
> Galilee, his brother PHILIP tetrarch of Iturea and Traconitis, and
> LYSANIAS tetrarch of Abilene—during the high priesthood of

ANNAS and CAIAPHAS, the word of God came to John son of Zachariah in the desert. (Luke 3:1–2, emphasis added)

In the Old Testament, God selected David—a young shepherd boy—after each of David's "all-pro" brothers had been paraded on the runway before the prophet Samuel. It was the lowly shepherd boy, David, whom God chose to be his anointed one.

The simple people that God chose to "hang with" were the first to recognize the unlikeliness of God's choice. No one summed up this surprise better than a simple woman from Nazareth who marveled that the "Mighty One" had "been mindful of the humble state of his servant" (Luke 1:48). Mary describes how God has "brought down rulers from their thrones but has lifted up the humble. He has filled the hungry with good things but has sent the rich away empty" (Luke 1:52–53). The first people to visit her newborn son were lowly shepherds (the kings came later). So, yes, while God loves all his children, he does seem to prefer hanging with the simple folks.

Does this mean that God "hates" rich people? No. In fact, it is important to note that Jesus never says that being rich is a sin. He does, however, warn of the dangers of riches, just as the prophets did throughout the Old Testament. God is not impressed with wealth but instead takes great joy in people who lead simple lives and who share their wealth with others. We can live simple lives and still be "rich."

Who are some people you admire because of the simple life they lead?

_____

_____

Don't Drink the Sand

What, then, is the danger of wealth? It is a mirage that fools us into thinking we are capable of sustaining ourselves at our deepest level. This mirage is the "original sin" according to the Judeo-Christian tradition, which tells the story of Adam and Eve and their attempt to sustain themselves ("become like God") by indulging in the "wealth" of the tree of knowledge of good and evil. It is a distortion and exploitation of God's creation.

We tend to associate the notion of a mirage with people wandering through the desert without any water. A mirage occurs when light passes through two layers of air which have different temperatures. The hot sun heats the sand and the heat that emanates from the sand heats the air just above it, causing light rays to bend and reflect the sky. When seen from a distance, this collision of air masses acts like a mirror reflecting the blue sky, which looks like a blue body of water. It is only as one gets closer and closer that the mirage evaporates, and one is left staring at nothing more than sand.

In a dramatic scene from the movie *The American President*, a presidential aide named Lewis (played by Michael J. Fox) confronts the president, Andrew Shepherd (played by Michael Douglas), about the need for authentic leadership. He says: "People want leadership, Mr. President, and in the absence of genuine leadership, they'll listen to anyone who steps up to the microphone. They want leadership. They're so thirsty for it they'll crawl through the desert toward a mirage, and when they discover there's no water, they'll drink the sand." In a cynical response, the president responds, "Lewis, we've had presidents who were beloved, who couldn't find a coherent sentence with two hands and a flashlight. People don't drink the sand because they're thirsty. They drink the sand because they don't know the difference."

Unfortunately, we are too often incapable of recognizing the difference between the mirage of wealth and the sustaining grace of God. It's okay to have wealth, but when we convince ourselves that our wealth, possessions, and status define and sustain us, we are essentially drinking the sand, mistaking it for living waters.

To what extent do wealth and possessions threaten to rule your life?

_____

_____

_____

Blessed Are the Poor in Spirit

This is precisely why Jesus proclaims in the Beatitudes that it is blessed to be poor in spirit (Mt 5:3). Being poor does not sound like a blessing; however, Jesus is emphasizing that those who are poor have no delusions about wealth sustaining them, since they have none. Jesus does not condemn those who are wealthy simply because they possess wealth. Instead, he uses the phrase "poor *in spirit*" because it is possible to have wealth but to fully recognize that it is not what ultimately sustains us.

Perhaps this is why *authentic* Christianity tends to be embraced more passionately in impoverished areas of the world than in affluent societies. I say "authentic" because, while Christianity does flourish among the affluent, it often morphs into the proclamation of a "prosperity gospel," which is the notion that God rewards with material wealth those who live faithful lives. It is difficult to proclaim a Savior to people who have everything and feel no need to be "saved" from anything.

So, what does God want of wealthy people? What are prosperous people supposed to do with all that wealth? Those of us in more affluent societies need to discover what it means to be people of faith amid wealth. We need to recognize our total dependence on God and the various forms of "poverty" we suffer (loneliness, despair, anxiety, etc.) despite all we possess. God wants those who are wealthy to share generously, recognizing that all of us are simply stewards of the treasures that have come our way. God created a world with abundant resources and intends for that abundance to be shared by all, not hoarded by a few. God wants those who are wealthy to be poor in spirit—knowing that God alone sustains us.

> Why do you think Christianity tends to be embraced more passionately in impoverished areas of the world? What is the "prosperity gospel," and how is it a distortion of the gospel of Jesus?
>
> _____
>
> _____
>
> _____

Our Need to Let Go

One of the most-loved books in recent Christian history is Henri Nouwen's *With Open Hands*. This seminal book begins with Nouwen telling the story of an elderly woman in a psychiatric ward who was frantically swinging at everything in sight. As the staff struggled to restrain her, they found that she was ferociously clinging to a small coin in her clenched fist. She was afraid that if they pried the coin—her last possession—from her hand, she would lose herself along with it. Nouwen goes on to say that the invitation to prayer—to enter a relationship with the Lord—is like being asked to open our tightly clenched fists and give up our last coin.

The truth is, we do tend to cling to our possessions as if they identify us, and we have a hard time letting go. They are called "possessions" for a good reason! In recent times, Marie Kondo has been attracting attention with her mission to encourage people to unclutter their lives. Her bottom line is, if a possession does not spark joy, get rid of it. It is this letting go that frees us from being owned by our material things. This notion is at the heart of the spirit of poverty that has been practiced by men and women in religious communities for centuries. Almsgiving—the giving of material goods to others—has always been considered one of the three central disciplines of discipleship along with prayer and fasting—disciplines that result in increased joy. As a Church, we annually mark the 40-day period of Lent, a time of tidying up and uncluttering our lives. Why do we do this? Because it leads to joy!

What is a possession you would have a hard time letting go of? What is a possession you did let go of, and how did it make you feel?

_____

_____

Many times I have heard from people who, having visited parts of the world where people live in extreme poverty, were astonished at the level of joy among those same people. And yet, for the many of us who live with the abundance of first-world countries, we hoard possessions and still struggle to be happy. There are even TV shows about this sad phenomenon.

To let go of something that we think defines us is to "die," to experience the death of a false self. The good news is that, in letting go, we can embrace the new life that the risen Christ—our true source of happiness and the One who defines us—offers us.

We would do well to take to heart the words of St. Ignatius of Loyola, who encouraged the attitude of *indifference*—not a lack of caring but an attitude of holding on loosely.

> For this it is necessary to make ourselves indifferent to all created things as much as we are able, so that we do not necessarily want health rather than sickness, riches rather than poverty, honor rather than dishonor, a long life rather than a short life, and so in all the rest, so that we ultimately desire and choose only what is most conducive for us to the end for which God created us. (The First Principle and Foundation, *The Spiritual Exercises*)

Indifference is the capacity to let go of what doesn't help us to love God or others while staying engaged with what does. Ignatius, like many other great saints, was the "Marie Kondo" of his time, encouraging us to hold on to only those things that "spark joy" while teaching that true joy is found only in our life with God.

How would you describe the Ignatian attitude of indifference? How do you seek to practice this attitude in your own life?

_____

_____

_____

Saint Francis of Assisi

One of the greatest and most dramatic examples in Christian history of this type of letting go is St. Francis of Assisi, who came from a wealthy family and who, in his youth, enjoyed the material comforts that came with wealthy living. Francis's father, a cloth merchant, fully expected Francis to be the heir to the lucrative family business. In his youth, Francis enjoyed the high life and sought to become a knight. After engaging in battle and ending up in prison for a year, Francis began to see things differently.

Before long, Francis abandoned his wealthy lifestyle and turned his attention to prayer and caring for those who were sick and poor. He took some cloth from his father's business, sold it, and used the money to repair a dilapidated church in response to a vision in which Jesus told him to "repair my church." His father was deeply troubled by this and sought to straighten out his son and get him back on track as an entrepreneur. In a dramatic climax to these efforts, Francis, in the presence of his father and the bishop, renounced his wealth and stripped naked, leaving behind his garments and his previous way of living.

Talk about letting go!

Francis went on to live a life of simplicity and poverty, giving birth to the Franciscan tradition and spirituality, which still influence countless people today, over 800 years later. While Francis's example is indeed radical, he exemplifies the call to authentic discipleship: to simplify our lives and not allow wealth to interfere with our responsibility to love and care for others.

> **What is it about St. Francis of Assisi that captures your imagination? How can his spirit of simplicity be practiced today?**
>
> _____
>
> _____
>
> _____

A Simple Pope

The influence of St. Francis of Assisi on Pope Francis was apparent from the moment he was elected and became the first pope to name himself after this great saint. Since the day he was elected pope, Pope Francis has taught, in word and action, that to follow Jesus means to live a life of simplicity. The world was enamored with the following examples of his simplicity and humility upon his election to the papacy in 2013:

- He appeared on the papal balcony for the first time after his election wearing only the white cassock and simple black shoes, eschewing the red cape with furry trim and the red shoes of his predecessors.

- He boarded the minibus with the other cardinals to head back to the hotel instead of being chauffeured in a papal limo.
- He went to the hotel desk to pay his own bill.
- He chose not to move into the papal palace but instead moved into the much simpler papal apartments.
- He continued to skip the papal limo in favor of a humbler Ford Focus.
- Images from his time in Buenos Aires show him riding public transportation on a regular basis.

It became clear that Pope Francis was communicating a new image for the Catholic Church: a simpler, more humble church that was closer to the poor of the world. Before long, he made news by "firing" a German bishop known as "Bishop Bling," who had reportedly spent over $40 million on his own residence. He did the same with a Brazilian bishop who had spent over $600,000 on renovations to his residence and offices. Pope Francis recognized that to live in the image of God, we need to live simply.

How do we go about simplifying our lives? It's a simple matter of subtraction.

What action of Pope Francis's most exemplifies to you his attitude of simplicity? Why do you think Pope Francis feels it is so important for the Church to project a simpler, humbler image?

_____

_____

Blessed by Less

In her book *Blessed by Less: Clearing Your Life of Clutter by Living Lightly*, Susan Vogt identifies several strategies for living more simply.

- eliminate clutter and excess possessions: Undertake the task of decluttering, not as an end in itself but as a way of passing on things you don't need anymore to those who can use them, thus opening yourself up to the needs of others.

- consume less: By reducing unnecessary consumption, we can simplify our lives while reducing the strain on the earth's resources.

- limit time spent on social media: Strive to be more present to the ordinary tasks of everyday living as well as to the spiritual wonder of humanity and nature.

- give away possessions: This practice reminds us that our existence, our identity, and our self-worth are about more than accumulating possessions and status. Giving away our "stuff" can also shift our attitudes toward possessions in general and help us clarify our true priorities.

- simplify your wardrobe: Purge your closet of clothing you haven't worn in months, outfits that don't fit, items that are no longer in style, to make your life simpler and less stressful.

- limit buying habits: Make purchases only after careful consideration and based on the extent to which the item(s) will add value to your life.

- eat out less and brown bag it more: While it's good to support your local restaurants, it is also true that eating out too often can turn into one of our biggest expenses.

- buy secondhand: This practice saves money, extends the life of the item, protects the environment, and reduces the power of consumerism over us.

- spend more time in nature: By communing with nature, we spend less time in stores, malls, and restaurants and, thus, spend less money and simplify our busy lives.
- purchase fair-trade products: By purchasing fair-trade products, we can reduce poverty, encourage production methods that are environmentally friendly, and promote humane working conditions.

Vogt emphasizes that living simply is a spiritual principle that is at the heart of Ignatian spirituality. She explains that for the six weeks of Lent some years ago, she decided to give away at least one item a day. When Lent ended, she realized that she still had more stuff than she needed, so she continued the practice for a year. When the year ended and she continued to find things that she was surprised she hadn't given away in earlier purges, her Lenten practice became a lifestyle.

Saint Ignatius of Loyola insisted that one of the keys to spiritual wellness is detachment from the things and worries of this world that might distract us from pursuing our ultimate purpose in life, which is to deepen our relationship with God. For us to "get up" like Elijah with renewed spiritual energy, we need to unload the excess baggage that burdens us and slows us down.

Which of the examples proposed by Susan Vogt for clearing your life of clutter most resonates with you? Why?

_____

_____

_____

The Simple Life "Ain't So Simple"!

Before we glibly wrap up this chapter on simplifying your life, it seems most appropriate to take into consideration a line from the Van Halen song "Runnin' with the Devil," which asserts that the simple life "ain't so simple." Living simply in today's complex world is not easy. Most of us have been conditioned by our culture to buy into all the "bells and whistles" that promise to make our lives better and ourselves more popular, thinner, younger-looking, more productive, and happier. To suddenly shift to a minimalist mentality that focuses on simplicity will bring us face-to-face with ourselves—and with the inner reality that life's clutter can keep us from getting in touch with. Likewise, there is nothing simple about raising children, maintaining healthy relationships, paying the bills, holding onto a job, living with chronic illness, or navigating through conflicts. We need to be careful not to confuse the simple life with an easy life.

The goal of a simple life is not to make things easier but to see more clearly, so that we can better differentiate between what is essential and what is not. When we reduce the clutter, we remove obstacles—mirages—so that we can recognize that which alone sustains us: the grace of God. To live a minimalist life is simply to recognize the mirages for what they are: delusions. We still need to find a true source of living water that will sustain us on the journey . . . lest we end up drinking the sand.

Why is it that living the simple life "ain't so simple"?

_____

_____

_____

In Summary . . .

God and those who speak on behalf of God—the Prophets—have always warned that material possessions can get in the way of encountering God and loving our neighbors. Throughout salvation history, God continually shows a preference for those who are poor and vulnerable, for those who live a simple life. We can become more fully human and tap into divine energy by simplifying our lives, reducing our possessions, and giving things away—all characteristic of a lifestyle that is pleasing to God.

Scripture Passages That Reveal/ Emphasize God's Love for Simplicity

The LORD is a refuge for the oppressed,
   a stronghold in times of trouble.
Psalm 9:9

"Because of the oppression of the weak
   and the groaning of the needy,
I will now arise," says the LORD.
   "I will protect them from those who malign them."
Psalm 12:5

I know that the LORD secures justice for the poor and upholds the cause of the needy.

Psalm 140:12

You have been a refuge for the poor,
    a refuge for the needy in his distress,
a shelter from the storm
    and a shade from the heat.

Isaiah 25:4

Blessed are the poor in spirit, for theirs is the kingdom of heaven.

Matthew 5:3

For where your treasure is, there your heart will be also.

Matthew 6:21

Which of the above Scripture quotes speaks to you most strongly about God's love of simplicity? Why?

_____

_____

As you reflect on this chapter, what is one shift you can make in your life to tap into the divine energy of simplicity?

_____

_____

Chapter 4

Build and Celebrate Relationships

To get the full value of joy you must have someone to divide it with.

—Mark Twain

In Search of Birth Parents

It is not uncommon for adoptees to go in search of their birth parents, seeking to learn more about their own identity: who they are, where they came from, and perhaps some insight into what traits they may have inherited. Even people who know their birth parents are spending time and money researching their genealogy to learn more about their heritage and identity.

As children of God, we also go in search of our Creator, hoping to learn more about what traits we have "inherited" from the Almighty. For thousands of years, disciples of Christ have held and taught (see the Apostles' Creed and the Nicene Creed) that the primary divine trait that God has revealed to us is God is Trinitarian: three Persons in One God.

"So, what does that have to do with me?" you may ask. "How can some arcane theological formula impact how I live from day to day?" Actually, it can and should have quite an impact on how we humans live.

The doctrine of the Trinity reveals a profound reality: God is intensely relational. The God in whose image we are made is a community of Persons—Father, Son, and Holy Spirit—whose love is so intimate that God is One. God's very essence is relational. If we hope to resemble God, in whose image and likeness we are made, and to be fully human, we must recognize, develop, embrace, and celebrate our relational nature.

Which relationships do you treasure most?

_____

_____

_____

It Is Not Good for Man to Be Alone

Remember what I said in chapter 1 about how some stories in the Bible are not intended to convey scientific or historical truth but rather spiritual truth? The second story of creation in the book of Genesis (chapter 2) is one such example. In this story God creates Adam and almost immediately says, "It is not good for the man to be alone" (Genesis 2:18). One of the very first things that God provides for Adam is a relationship. This is significant because parents always want to share with their children what they themselves treasure most. In this case, God wants his children to experience and enjoy the same kind of intimacy that the Trinity enjoys: an intimacy so profound that Three Persons are One. The creation of Adam, then of Eve as his companion, reveals that God considers relationships to be necessary for our human welfare. From that point on, the Bible unfolds as a compendium of stories essentially about relationships. When you think about it, many of the most well-known Bible stories are named in reference to the relationship in the story:

Adam and Eve	Ruth and Boaz
Cain and Abel	David and Goliath
Abraham and Sarah	David and Jonathan
Sarah and Hagar	David and Bathsheba
Isaac and Ishmael	Mary and Joseph
Abraham and Isaac	Martha and Mary
Isaac and Rebekah	Jesus, Mary, Martha, and Lazarus
Jacob and Esau	Jesus and Zacchaeus
Joseph and his brothers	Jesus and the Pharisees
Moses and Aaron	Jesus and the Twelve
Moses and Miriam	Jesus and Peter, James, and John
Samson and Delilah	Jesus and Pilate
Ruth and Naomi	Paul and Barnabas

Which of the above relationship stories are you most familiar with? Which is your favorite? Why?

_____

_____

_____

Likewise, many of Jesus' most famous parables tell stories of relationships: The Good Samaritan (a story about the relationship between a Samaritan and a man—assumed to be a Jew—who fell victim to robbers), The Prodigal Son (a story about the relationship between a father and his two sons), and The Last Judgment (a story of the relationships we have with those who are poor, hungry, thirsty, naked, homeless, sick, and in prison). Repeatedly, Scripture reveals that God places great importance on relationships.

God knew something that humankind has learned over time: it is generally not good for us humans to be alone—that is, isolated from others. Even introverts need relationships! In fact, research done over many decades indicates that isolation and loneliness are associated with weakened immune systems, chronic inflammation, high blood pressure, and many other health issues, including mental and emotional health. At the same time, studies reveal that people with strong social networks experience reduced physical symptoms of stress (especially pain), tend to live longer, and experience greater levels of happiness.

During the COVID-19 pandemic, people all over the world experienced an extended period of intense isolation as social distancing and secure-at-home policies were enforced. Many people quickly came to realize just how much they rely on social interaction and relationships in day-to-day living and sought creative ways of connecting with others—virtual happy hours, increased FaceTime, Zoom gatherings, and watch parties—anything to maintain social connection while respecting physical distancing. Being apart is one thing; being alone is another.

When have you been forced to experience isolation? What was that experience like? How can/do you stay connected with people even when you are physically apart?

_____

_____

Seven Out of Ten

Even the Ten Commandments are about relationships. Have you ever noticed that only three are about our relationship with God, while seven are about relationships with our neighbors? The first through the third commandments direct us to "get right" in our relationship with God, requiring us to worship God alone, not to take God's name in vain, and to keep holy the sabbath day. Commandments four through ten then direct us to get right with our neighbors, requiring us to honor our parents and not do the following to our neighbors: kill, commit adultery, steal, bear false witness, covet their goods, and covet their spouse. This reveals something critically important about God: God is most interested in how we love one another and insists that love of God and love of neighbor cannot be separated. God is saying that the greatest way to show our love for him is by showing love for our neighbor.

It is no accident, then, that Jesus responded to a question about which of the commandments is most important by insisting, "'Love the Lord your God with all your heart and with all your soul and with all your mind.' This is the first and greatest commandment. And the second is like it: 'Love your neighbor as yourself'" (Matthew 22:37–39). The heart of the Law is relationships! In many ways, the Bible can serve as a relationship manual, because so many of its passages are concerned with teaching us how to deepen, nurture, protect, and enjoy healthy relationships. After all, the author of the Bible—God, speaking through human voices—is intensely relational. We tend to think of the Bible as prescribing endless and seemingly arbitrary rules and restrictions about ethical behavior, but such rules are present because God is primarily interested in sustaining relationships. The essence of discipleship is entering a relationship with God (through Jesus Christ) and with his people.

In what ways can the Bible be thought of as a relationship manual?

_____

_____

_____

Relationships Require Work

If relationships were easy, we would not need an entire Bible (or countless numbers of self-help books on relationships) to teach us how to navigate them! We might recognize the need for relationships and desire to form healthy relationships, but it's not easy—in fact, relationships can be a major source of pain and frustration. It is for this reason that we have something called "relationship coaches"—people who help others identify their relationship problems, chart paths for mutual understanding, identify strategies and tools for strengthening relationships, and acquire skills for cultivating honest communication, respect, and intimacy.

My wife and I are now grandparents, and our lives are enriched by toddlers. They remind us a lot about how to behave and not behave. As I pondered the topic of this chapter, it occurred to me that right in front of me (at knee height, you understand) were living illustrations of what it takes to maintain a relationship. Let me explain.

Whenever two or more toddlers are placed together under adult supervision, sooner or later you will hear the following admonishments:

- "Share!" (in reference to one toddler grabbing a toy and yelling, "Mine!")
- "Leave him/her alone!" (in reference to one toddler invading the space of another)
- "Listen to me!" (in reference to one or more toddlers ignoring directions)
- "Get back here!" (in reference to one or more toddlers venturing where they should not venture)
- "Say hi!" (in reference to one toddler being introduced to another for the first time)
- "No, no, no . . . we don't do that!" (in reference to one or more toddlers doing something unacceptable)

In these six statements are the key strategies for maintaining healthy relationships throughout all of life! Let's take a look.

Which of the above statements have you heard yourself (or others) say when speaking to a toddler/group of toddlers? What type(s) of situation(s) led to this admonition and how is this behavior still manifested in adult relationships?

_____

_____

_____

"Share!"

When toddlers play together, inevitably one of them grabs a toy that the other is holding, and all hell breaks loose! In response, the caregiver says, "Share!" Relationships thrive on generous sharing. No relationship will survive if one or more of the parties is selfish when it comes to sharing material goods. The healthiest relationships are fed by a spirit of generosity in which both parties freely share with one another and even go as far as putting the well-being of the other before their own needs.

In all our relationships, we are called to practice this spirit of sharing. In healthy marriages and families, fewer things are thought of as "mine" and more as "ours." In friendships, generous and selfless sharing nurtures the bond of the relationship. Socially, our world is a more just place in which to live if material goods are shared fairly. To resemble God and to tap into divine energy, we are called to share, because God shared his only Son, Jesus, with us.

> **Describe a relationship of yours in which you do a great deal of sharing. How does this sharing contribute to your relationship?**
>
> _____
>
> _____
>
> _____

"Leave him/her alone!"

Toddlers cannot keep their hands to themselves. Inevitably, one of them will reach out and scratch, slap, hit, grab, bite, or poke the other, to which the caregiver responds by saying, "Leave him/her alone!" The toddlers are being taught to respect boundaries and to respect another person's space and body. All relationships have boundaries and, if a relationship is to thrive, those boundaries must be respected.

Boundaries are a means of protecting that which is sacred. As children of God made in the image and likeness of God, we recognize each person and each relationship as sacred: as an opportunity to experience the divine life, which is relational. In response, we honor boundaries as a way of honoring the other. To help us resemble God and tap into divine energy, the Holy Spirit enables us to work at building healthy relationships. Spend time with people you love. Enjoy the company of others. And truly, truly, love your neighbor as yourself, which means respecting boundaries.

> **What role do boundaries play in your relationships? How do boundaries differ in your relationships? How have you needed to renegotiate or establish new boundaries in order to repair a relationship?**
>
> _____
>
> _____
>
> _____

"Listen to me!"

Toddlers have a way of pushing the envelope and exerting their autonomy. While that is a good thing and a natural part of development, it also requires the adult in the room to occasionally assert authority to remind them that they are not free to do as they please. They may not like this, but it's how they learn that they must listen to and consider the voice of another when making decisions and choices. They learn accountability.

Healthy relationships thrive on mutual accountability. Both parties recognize and share a common goal and commit to contributing equitably toward the achievement of that goal. In our relationships, we are called to listen—to our own voice, to the voice of others, and to the voice of God. Relationships require that we act as members of a partnership, engaging in honest communication and remaining accountable to one another. To share in divine energy is to share in a community of Three Persons whose essence is complete mutuality.

To whom are you accountable? Who is accountable to you? How can mutual accountability strengthen your relationships?

_____

_____

_____

"Get back here!"

Anyone caring for children will tell you that if you turn your back on a toddler for just a few seconds, they will scamper where they're not supposed to go. "Get back here!" are words that few caregivers can avoid. Toddlers are notorious for NOT remaining in one place.

All healthy relationships require stability. When a conflict arises in a relationship, we may be tempted to simply avoid the individual and move to another relationship. In doing so, however, we never learn how to work through and resolve conflicts. Any relationship worth salvaging beckons us to "get back here" and work things out. Stability is a trait that enables us to work at relationships that are experiencing difficulties but can be salvaged. Of course, it goes without saying that no one is required to stay in a relationship that is abusive or toxic. Stability is not a life sentence that imprisons us in an unhealthy environment.

> **Describe a relationship of yours in which you have practiced stability (you have remained to work through conflicts).**
>
> _____
>
> _____
>
> _____

"Say hi!"

It can be comical to watch a toddler arriving for a playdate with someone he or she is meeting for the first time. They approach very cautiously and gaze suspiciously at their blind date. The adults realize that they need to step in to make things happen, prompting the children to "Say hi!" to one another to establish basic civility and hospitality. Children are taught to welcome guests into their space.

In our relationships, we sometimes underemphasize hospitality. Very simply, hospitality is characterized by generously and warmly welcoming and receiving others. This is something we can and should do at home, at work, in social situations, when we're shopping, when we're commuting—in just about any situation. Hospitality is a way of connecting with others. It is a way of putting the needs of others before our own. It is a way of making space for others. Hospitality literally opens doors to the possibility of relationship. We are called to practice hospitality, not just when meeting people for the first time but each time we encounter them. It is interesting to note that all three of the great "Abrahamic" religions—Judaism, Christianity, and Islam—view hospitality and civility as a minimum requirement, as encapsulated in the story of Abraham and Sarah welcoming the three strangers in Genesis 18.

How, when, and to whom do you practice hospitality? Who shows great hospitality to you?

_____

_____

_____

"No, no, no . . . we don't do that!"

Toddlers find all kinds of ways to get into trouble. Parents and caregivers find themselves in the position of correcting young children, pointing out actions that are right from those that are wrong. In essence, parents and caregivers begin teaching virtues to their children at a very young age in hopes that they will learn right from wrong and will break bad habits and form good ones. We teach them that character matters and that they should strive to grow in habits of virtue while avoiding bad habits. And we do not hesitate to correct them and to point out behaviors that are unbecoming of them.

We need people who can be honest with us—people who help us "keep it real"—to be humble, authentic, and not "puffed up," to borrow a phrase from St. Paul (1 Corinthians 4:6, NRSV). It is through healthy relationships that we experience growth in virtues. We said earlier that "God creates and God restores." Honest and healthy relationships restore us when we veer off track, enabling us to grow into the person God intends us to be.

Describe a relationship that has helped you grow as a person. How does this person help you to "keep it real"?

_____

_____

_____

Relationships Need Rules

In our increasingly individualistic and libertarian society, rules are not very popular. We are conditioned to see rules as unwanted limits. The truth is, rules protect that which we value most. Healthy relationships require rules, and we establish those rules with one another all the time. For example: you make a new acquaintance, and her name is Kathleen, so the next time you see her you say, "Hey, Katie, how are you?" only to be reprimanded, "Please don't call me Katie. This creep at school used to call me that and I always hated it." Bam!—a rule has been established, and if you want that relationship to develop further, you will honor that rule.

Rules also free us to excel at something we may otherwise struggle at. For example, if you want to excel at fishing, it helps to get some advice from someone more experienced who can provide "rules" for the best time to fish, such as the best location, the best way to bait your hook, the best kind of equipment, and the best techniques. All of these guidelines will free you to enjoy the experience of fishing instead of being bogged down by a trial-and-error approach.

In the same way, if we want to be free to enjoy relationships, it behooves us to follow some simple rules—most of which we were taught when we were toddlers.

> **What are some rules that you observe in a significant relationship in your life? How did these rules develop or get established? Were they explicitly stated, or did they simply evolve as the relationship evolved?**
>
> _____
>
> _____

The Ultimate Example of Relationship Rules

Perhaps the best example of the need for rules in relationships comes from the successful experience of Benedictine monasteries. Until the fifth century, those in religious life basically lived as hermits. With the fall of the Roman Empire and the dissolution of societal structures and communities, monasteries became beacons of communal life, striving to show how people needed healthy relationships to survive as a society. To make this happen, St. Benedict established his Rule, which for over fifteen hundred years has enabled countless numbers of men and women in religious life to enjoy the benefits of healthy relationships. He did this by requiring members of the community to follow rules that, for all intents and purposes, we strive to teach toddlers.

- Share–through a life of poverty, members of the community learn to share all things in common and to be detached from material possessions.

- "Leave him/her alone!"–through a life of chastity, members learn to respect boundaries, both emotional and physical.

- "Listen to me!"–through a life of obedience, members learn to live in mutual accountability with one another and to legitimate authority.

- "Get back here!"–through a life of stability, members learn to remain where they are and to work through conflicts that arise with other members.

- "Say hi!"–through a life of hospitality, members learn to greet each guest as if he/she were Christ.

- "No, no, no . . . we don't do that!"–through a life that is committed to ongoing conversion, members help one another to grow in virtue.

Just how successful are such communities that follow the Rule of St. Benedict (or some variation thereof)? A recent study revealed that religious sisters experience greater physical and emotional well-being at the end of life than other women and are 27 percent more likely to live into their seventies. The study identified six reasons for this phenomenon: the sisters keep moving, they practice positive emotions, they have a purpose and work for it, they maintain community (healthy relationships), they have little to no fear of death, and they let go of attachments (Anna Corwin, The Nun Study).

I remember talking to my friend Tom McLaughlin, years before he passed away, about his experience of living as a monk for a few years early in his adulthood. He said, "It was the most authentic experience of relationships I ever had. There was total honesty. In fact, it was so honest, they convinced me that God was not calling me to live as a monk!" Perhaps we can all learn from toddlers and monks about the rules we need to follow if we hope to have healthy relationships in our lives and, thus, to resemble God and be spiritually alive!

What can you learn about relationships from the lives of men and women religious who live the monastic life?

_____

_____

_____

Family Relationships

For most of us, our "schooling" in the rules of relationships occurs in our family. Building upon the thoughts and words of his predecessor, St. Pope John Paul II, Pope Francis characterized the family as the "first school of love" as well as the "first school of mercy." Both Holy Fathers are drawing from the *Catechism of the Catholic Church,* which states clearly that the family is "a community of grace and prayer, a school of human virtues and of Christian charity" (1666).

At times, "church talk" about families can become idealistic and romanticized. Pope Francis made it clear, however, that "the Holy Family of holy cards does not exist" (*Angelus* reflection, Feast of the Holy Family, 2021). Family life is, in reality, complex and messy. And yet, it is in that very real situation that we learn how to build, navigate, and sustain relationships. Many of the virtues that we learn in family life—acceptance, affection, patience, understanding, compassion, empathy, responsibility, gratitude, and conflict resolution, to name a few—assist us in forming, building, navigating, and sustaining relationships throughout life.

What relationship skills/virtues did you learn from your family experience? What relationship skills/virtues were missing from your family experience, and where/how/from whom did you attain them?

_____

_____

_____

Living as People for Others

When I attended St. Ignatius College Prep back in the day, I remember being taught by the Jesuits that we were to be "men for others" (it was an all-boys school). Years later, when I began working at Loyola Press, I found out that we had a committee called "People for Others," which was committed to providing opportunities for employees to actively show love of neighbor, especially those in need. It turns out that being a "person for others" is a hallmark of Ignatian spirituality, grounded in the belief that we have been created by God to live in relationship with all people—even those we will never meet.

If we hope to resemble God and tap into divine energy, we need to be "people for others" because being "for others" is what God is all about: "For God so loved the world that he gave his one and only Son, that whoever believes in him shall not perish but have eternal life" (John 3:16). For God, it is all about relationships.

How do you attempt to live as a "person for others"?

_____

_____

_____

Relationships Keep Us Healthy

Research reveals that people with healthy relationships have fewer doctor visits, shorter hospital stays, and more positive emotions. In fact, the health benefits of healthy relationships include the following:

longer life span
stronger immune system
quicker healing
lower blood pressure
better physical fitness
healthier behaviors
healthier heart

less pain
less stress and anxiety
less depression and sub-
  stance abuse
fewer colds
better sleep

Having several strong, healthy relationships in your life can have a profound impact on your physical, mental, and spiritual health.

> **What is/are the most positive, strong, and healthy relationship(s) in your life? Which of the above health benefits might you be enjoying because of this/these healthy relationship(s)?**
>
> _____
>
> _____
>
> _____

Celebrate Your Relationships

Of the many features that Facebook offers, one is a notification of your "friendversary," a message that reminds you of the date that you and someone else became Facebook friends so that you can celebrate the relationship. One of the best ways to keep a relationship healthy is to celebrate it. A good way to do this is to establish relationship rituals. A ritual is an act that is performed in a regular and set way with mindfulness (as opposed to a routine, which is done mindlessly).

Relationship rituals might include getting together regularly to share a meal, a cup of coffee or a happy hour at a specific location, engaging in a hobby together, marking important events (birthdays, anniversaries), greeting or saying good-bye to one another in a specific way (a hug, kiss, phrase), checking in with each other on a regular basis, or following a pattern of discussion that enables each person to share joys, sorrows, successes, and failures. Such rituals create a sense of connection, provoke and promote the sharing of emotions, provide structure for expression of affection, create a desirable mood or climate for the relationship, facilitate reconciliation, and reinforce a strong sense of "we-ness." The Holy Spirit prompts us to enjoy our relationships. The more we work at them, the more we share in divine energy.

What are some relationship rituals that you share with others? How do you celebrate your relationships?

_____

_____

_____

Relationships and Fun

Fun tends to get a bad rap in a world that places far too much emphasis on being productive. Too often, fun is thought of as frivolous, as something that serious people should not waste too much time on. The truth is, fun is not only good for us but also necessary for our overall health—mental, physical, emotional, and spiritual. And one of the most important venues for experiencing fun is within relationships. In her book *The Power of Fun: How to Feel Alive Again*, health and science journalist Catherine Price contends that fun is the key to coming "back to life" when one finds oneself languishing.

Price explains that fun can be an elusive concept, and she distinguishes between what she calls "fake fun" (social media, binge-watching TV, etc.) and "true fun," which is characterized by three key ingredients: playfulness (a spirit of lightheartedness and freedom), connection (having a shared experience with someone), and flow (being fully engaged and focused). Price points out that, while there is little scientific research about the potential health benefits of fun (namely because we have not had a good definition of fun), there is ample research on the benefits of playfulness, connection, and flow—all three of which have been shown to have positive effects on mental and physical health.

If spiritual health can be likened to feeling truly alive, then engaging in fun can most certainly be thought of as a spiritual experience. Certainly, God wants us to do some serious and important things with and in our lives, but he also wants us to have joy and to spread joy, hope, and love to others. We stand little chance of doing that successfully if we are "no fun." And fun is multiplied when the activity is shared with others. So, if you want to have a positive spiritual experience, get together with some good friends or family members and have some fun! And if you want to be an effective and authentic proclaimer of the gospel—of "good news"—be sure to show people that you know how to have fun.

When was the last time you truly had fun (felt alive, connected, lighthearted, exhilarated)? Describe the experience. How did being in relationship with others/another contribute to this overall feeling?

_____

_____

_____

In Summary . . .

God is all about forming community and, in the Christian tradition, God IS community (the Trinity: Father, Son, and Holy Spirit). So much of divine revelation (in particular, sacred Scripture) is concerned with protecting relationships. We can become more fully human and tap into divine energy by fostering community, building, sustaining, and celebrating our relationships.

Scripture Passages That Reveal/ Emphasize God's Relationality

It is not good for the man to be alone.
Genesis 2:18

How good and pleasant it is
   when brothers live together in unity!
Psalm 133:1

Faithful friends are a sturdy shelter:
  whoever finds one has found a treasure.
Faithful friends are beyond price;
  no amount can balance their worth.
Faithful friends are life-saving medicine;
  and those who fear the Lord will find them.
Sirach 6:14–16 (NRSVCE)

I was a stranger and you invited me in.
Matthew 25:35

I appeal to you, brothers, in the name of our Lord Jesus Christ, that all of you agree with one another so that there may be no divisions among you and that you may be perfectly united in mind and thought.
1 Corinthians 1:10

For anyone who does not love his brother, whom he can see, cannot love God, whom he has not seen.
1 John 4:20

Which of the above Scripture quotes speaks to you most strongly about God's relationality? Why?

_____

_____

_____

As you reflect on this chapter, what is one shift you can make in your life to tap into the divine energy of celebrating relationships?

_____

_____

_____

Chapter 5

Show Compassion

Love and compassion are necessities, not luxuries. Without them,
humanity cannot survive.

—Dalai Lama

The Wrath of God?

It is unfortunate that many of us have been given the erroneous impression that the God of the Old Testament was a God of wrath and the God of the New Testament was a God of peace and love. While it's true that the Old Testament does attribute a fair amount of "smiting" to God, such wrath was directed at those who lived in opposition to God's goodness. Likewise, it was customary to label the misfortunes of one's enemies as the "wrath of God" (something that some misguided people still do today). If, however, we want to know whether the God of the Old Testament was truly wrathful, we should look to what his first children—the Jewish people—have said about him over thousands of years. And what will you find? In Scripture, the Jewish people repeatedly refer to God as "gracious and compassionate, slow to anger and rich in love" (see Exodus 34:6; Numbers 14:18; Nehemiah 9:17; Psalms 86:15, 103:8, 145:8; Joel 2:13; Jonah 4:2; Nahum 1:3).

The seminal moment in the Old Testament—the Exodus event—is a story of God's compassion for vulnerable people: "I have indeed seen the misery of my people in Egypt. I have heard them crying out because of their slave drivers, and I am concerned about their suffering" (Exodus 3:7). The story proceeds to describe how God, through Moses, led the Jewish people out of slavery in Egypt to freedom in the Promised Land and protected them along the way of their difficult journey, providing water from the rock, manna from heaven, and guidance through a pillar of fire by night and a pillar of cloud by day, all because he was "concerned about their suffering." In fact, the Jewish people's experience of God's compassion was so prominent that the prophets of Israel called on the Jewish people to resemble their God and to be compassionate to those who are vulnerable.

> **Describe a time in your life when you were struggling/suffering and someone stepped forward to assist you because they were concerned about you.**
>
> _____
>
> _____
>
> _____

It's interesting to note that, throughout the rest of the Old Testament, God often identifies himself by recalling this act of compassion: "I am the LORD your God, who brought you out of Egypt, out of the land of slavery" (Exodus 20:2). This, of course, is the passage that forms the basis of the first commandment, which we know as "I am the

Lord your God. You shall have no other gods before me." The whole passage actually reads: "I am the LORD your God, who brought you out of Egypt, out of the land of slavery. You shall have no other gods before me" (Exodus 20:2–3). The first commandment, which "introduces" us to God, introduces him as a God who is known by his compassionate actions. Like any parent, God reminds his children what he has done for them, gently nudging them to show a little respect and appreciation in return and to pay it forward to others!

Up to this very day, the Jewish people identify God with this compassionate act. In the Passover seder meal, when the youngest person in the household asks, "Why is tonight different from all other nights?" the response is to tell the story of God's compassionate act: "We were slaves to Pharaoh in Egypt, and God brought us out with a strong hand and an outstretched arm." Every year, the Jewish people celebrate the fact that they came to know who God is and who they are as a people, through God's act of compassion in the Exodus story.

Identify something your parents did for your well-being that they often (or even occasionally) have reminded you about. Have you ever felt compelled to remind someone (your children, your spouse, a friend, a family member) of something good you did for them?

_____

_____

_____

The God of Compassion

Even in the stories of their prehistory, the Jewish people speak of a God who is compassionate. After Adam and Eve disobeyed God and paid the consequences by being driven from the Garden of Eden, the very next thing God did was to tenderly sew together some skins to clothe them and protect them from the elements since they were naked (Genesis 3:21). Likewise, after Cain killed his brother Abel and faced the consequences of being banished to a foreign land, God placed a mark on Cain to protect him from anyone seeking vengeance (Genesis 4:15). Neither of those actions portrays God as wrathful. Story after story in the Old Testament shows that while there are consequences for going against God's Law of love, God's justice is accompanied by generous compassion.

Everything the Jewish people learned from their experience of God pointed to a realization that became clear with the coming of Jesus Christ, who is the embodiment of God's compassion. Throughout the four Gospels, we encounter a Christ who is driven by compassion as he reaches out to the most vulnerable: those who are sick, poor, mourning, widowed, and so on. In fact, the Gospels tell us that compassion drives Jesus to

- cure unnamed illnesses (Matthew 9:36; 14:14)
- multiply the loaves and fishes (Matthew 15:32)
- heal a blind person (Matthew 20:34)
- cure lepers (Mark 1:41)
- drive a demon out of a boy (Mark 9:22)
- raise a boy from the dead (Luke 7:13)

Perhaps Jesus' compassionate stance toward others is best captured in this passage from the Gospel of Mark: "When Jesus landed and saw a large crowd, he had compassion on them, because they were like sheep without a shepherd. So he began teaching them many things" (Mark 6:34). The Gospels, and all of Scripture for that matter, teach us that compassion is not just some warm and fuzzy feeling that God gets every so often but that it is a divine attribute. Jesus himself said, "Be compassionate as my Father in heaven is compassionate" (Luke 6:36, NLT). This means that, for a life of true discipleship, compassion is nonnegotiable: we are obligated to cultivate a compassionate approach to life. Each of us will become more recognizable as a child of God, made in God's image and likeness, if we show compassion, especially for those in need.

Of course, Jesus' ultimate act of compassion was his suffering and death on the cross so that, through his resurrection and the sending of the Holy Spirit, we might be saved from sin. No matter how much suffering we experience in this life, we know that our God understands because he became one of us and suffered and died in the most selfless and compassionate act imaginable: laying down his life for others.

What is your favorite Gospel story of Jesus showing compassion for someone or for some group of people? Why?

_____

_____

_____

Compassion Begins with Empathy

Empathy is the consequence of being in relationship to others, which means that everything another person experiences somehow involves me. While compassion and empathy are closely related, they are not the same thing. Empathy is the ability to recognize that someone is suffering and to feel what they feel. That, however, can be done from a distance. Compassion, on the other hand, is when we feel another's suffering so strongly that we are compelled to reduce, alleviate, or eliminate it through some course of action. While empathy is felt in the heart, compassion is felt in the gut. In fact, the Greek word used in the New Testament for "compassion"—*splanchnizomai*—is structured on the root word, *splanch* or *splanchna*, which means "guts." In other words, it literally takes guts to be compassionate. A truly compassionate response is visceral: it is felt so deeply that it moves us to action.

This is the kind of compassion that is portrayed in the story of the Good Samaritan. It is quite possible that the priest and the Levite had *empathy* for the injured man. However, it was the Samaritan who felt it in his gut and was moved to action. That's compassion. And Jesus presents it as the same kind of compassion that God has for his people. He is saying that the Samaritan resembles God more than the priest and the Levite. No wonder some in his Jewish audience—those who saw themselves as God's very own children—were so angered at his stories and at Jesus' suggestion that an outcast (a Samaritan) could resemble God more than they themselves. Jesus makes it clear, however, that radical compassion is integral to a life of discipleship.

In your life, what is the relationship between empathy and compassion?

_____

_____

_____

What Compassion Is and Is Not

Compassion is too often thought of as a pious, sentimental human feeling that romanticizes the pain and suffering of others. While compassion involves affect, it is not a fleeting sentiment. Rather, it is an affective approach to all of life that enables one to view the pain and suffering of others as one's own. This "stance" toward life enables one to stand in solidarity with others—not just feeling empathy for their pain and suffering but, rather, identifying with those who are suffering and vulnerable, most especially when that suffering is undeserved. Perhaps that is why people who themselves have been deeply wounded are often capable of practicing the greatest compassion.

As with most things spiritual or religious, we need not overdramatize what it means to show compassion to others. While it's true that people such as St. Mother Teresa of Calcutta and Dorothy Day are great examples of compassion, each of us is called to show compassion in everyday, undramatic ways, many of which we are already doing. If compassion can be understood as being moved to action over someone's need or suffering, then the following everyday actions are examples of compassion in action:

- waking up in the middle of the night to feed and change the diaper of your crying baby
- stooping down to pick up and cradle a toddler who is crying
- taking a friend out for a cup of coffee or a bite to eat to talk about his or her struggles
- chipping in to assist a coworker in completing a project he or she is having difficulty with
- spending some extra time with a struggling teenager (or attending an event they are participating/performing in)
- surprising your spouse by unexpectedly completing a chore they felt overwhelmed by
- offering a ride to a friend who has errands or medical appointments but cannot drive
- picking up a few groceries for a friend who is trying to keep up with a busy schedule that is pulling them in different directions
- reaching up to get an item off a high shelf at the grocery store for an elderly or incapacitated person
- holding a door open for someone who is carrying things or pushing a stroller
- offering to help a neighbor complete a chore that is difficult for them to handle alone
- letting someone with fewer items get in front of you at the supermarket
- going out of your way to make a newcomer feel welcomed
- helping an elderly or pregnant neighbor unload their groceries
- leaving a generous tip for a hardworking restaurant server or hotel worker
- watching someone's kids so they can run errands or just take a break

- retrieving your neighbor's garbage receptacle from the curb after pick-up
- shoveling snow in front of a neighbor's house
- writing a glowing letter of recommendation or helping set up an interview for someone struggling to land a job
- sharing your umbrella with someone in a downpour
- giving up your seat on public transportation for someone who is elderly, disabled, or just looking tired or burdened
- sending a message of affirmation to an employee, a coworker, or an employer who is doing their best but is overwhelmed by the workload
- offering to carpool to work or to drive a neighbor's kids to school
- watching a neighbor's child after school until one of the parents gets home from work
- participating in peaceful protests/standing in solidarity with people whose rights are not being respected

This list could go on, and I'm sure you can see yourself doing a number of these things if you're not already doing so. They are everyday actions that result from noticing someone else's struggle and putting aside your own needs to ease their burden. That's called "laying down your life" for others, something that Jesus said is the greatest love a person can have: a love that is compassionate.

In the spirit of the list above and in all humility, think of and describe three simple acts of compassion that you have performed for others in the past few days. Then, think of at least one simple act of compassion that you were the beneficiary of. How did that action make you feel?

_____

_____

_____

Compassion and True Happiness

We live in a society that claims we can achieve happiness by amassing possessions. And while material possessions may very well bring us some instant gratification, research is showing that true happiness is achieved by practicing compassion: helping others, giving without expecting anything in return, and treating others as an "other self." For example,

- The Corporation for National and Community Service reports that people are 33 percent less likely to identify as unhealthy if they volunteer for 100 hours of service per year.

- Harvard Business School professor Michael Norton published a study in *Science* in which participants were given a sum of money; half were told to spend the money on themselves while half were told to spend it on others. Those who spent the money on others reported higher levels of happiness than those who spent it on themselves.

- Researchers in Great Britain report in the *Journal of Social Psychology* that participants in a study who were directed to do acts of kindness for ten days increased scores on a happiness survey, while those participants who received no instructions for how to spend the ten days showed no increase in the happiness survey.

- A study by Sara Konrath of the University of Michigan reveals that people who engaged in volunteerism (for altruistic reasons) lived longer than peers who did not volunteer.

These examples are just the tip of the iceberg of growing research that shows that being compassionate has benefits for our health and well-being and perhaps may be as necessary for good health as diet and exercise. Showing compassion toward others is indeed a powerful way of tapping into divine energy.

Describe how you feel after performing a significant act of compassion.

_____

_____

_____

Compassion and Contemplation

In 1987, Franciscan priest and well-known speaker/author Fr. Richard Rohr founded the Center for Action and Contemplation in Albuquerque, New Mexico. He has said that the most important word in the Center's title is the word *and*, explaining that we need both compassionate action *and* contemplative practice for the spiritual journey. Rohr reasons that without contemplative prayer, we run the risk of our action flowing from our ego rather than from true compassion and that, without compassionate action, any contemplative prayer is incomplete and self-centered. It does not matter which comes first, but the two are reliant on each other.

Contemplation is not just some esoteric form of navel-gazing. Nor is it an attempt to escape the realities of this life and experience "nothingness." Contemplation puts us in touch with ourselves, including our own brokenness, so that the Lord might lead us to become more sensitive—more compassionate—to the needs of others. In fact, in Matthew 25, Jesus makes it clear that our final judgment will be measured by the extent to which we showed compassion to others: those who are hungry, thirsty, naked, homeless, imprisoned, and so on. Anglican Archbishop Rowan Williams summed this up beautifully when he said that contemplation is not the search for "some private 'religious experience' that will make us feel secure or holy. We seek it because in this self-forgetting gazing towards the light of God in Christ we learn how to look at one another and at the whole of God's creation" (Address to the Synod of Bishops on The New Evangelization, 2012).

In prayer, we call to mind those who are suffering and ask God for the grace to move from empathy to compassionate action. And the first step toward making this happen is to present ourselves to our compassionate God and ask for his help with our own brokenness. This need explains why the Mass begins with the assembly praying for forgiveness in the Penitential Act and why the Liturgy of the Hours begins with the words "God, come to my assistance. Lord, make haste to help me." We need help and we, in turn, are called to help others. Just as we seek God's compassionate activity in our lives, we are called to respond—to embody this divine attribute—by acting to help others. Such is the nature of true compassion and true discipleship.

How can/do compassion and contemplation work together in your life? Why are both necessary?

_____

_____

_____

In Summary . . .

One of the most evident divine attributes is compassion for those who are suffering or vulnerable. The Jewish people characterized God as "gracious and compassionate, slow to anger and abounding in love." Jesus Christ is the embodiment of God's compassion. We can become more fully human and tap into divine energy by accompanying those in need and responding to their needs with compassion.

Scripture Passages That Reveal/ Emphasize God's Compassion

When he cries out to me, I will hear, for I am compassionate.
Exodus 22:27

But the LORD was gracious to them and had compassion and showed concern for them because of his covenant with Abraham, Isaac and Jacob.
2 Kings 13:23

The LORD is good to all;
>   he has compassion on all he has made.
Psalm 145:9

Yet the LORD longs to be gracious to you;
>   he rises to show you compassion.
For the LORD is a God of justice.
>   Blessed are all who wait for him!
Isaiah 30:18

They will neither hunger nor thirst,
>   nor will the desert heat or the sun beat down upon them.
He who has compassion on them will guide them
>   and lead them beside springs of water.
Isaiah 49:10

When he saw the crowds, he had compassion on them, because they were harassed and helpless, like sheep without a shepherd.
Matthew 9:36

Which of the above Scripture quotes speaks to you most strongly about God's compassion? Why?

_____

_____

_____

As you reflect on this chapter, what is one shift you can make in your life to tap into the divine energy of compassion?

_____

_____

_____

Chapter 6
Make Repairs

By a Carpenter mankind was made, and only by that Carpenter
can mankind be remade.
—Desiderius Erasmus

Fixer-Upper

We human beings tend to enjoy watching repairs. Construction sites have "viewing panels" in the fence around the site so that inspectors can have easy access to viewing; however, these peepholes are most often used by everyday pedestrians who just want to catch a glimpse of something being built or repaired. HGTV, a cable TV network, makes a living from showing homes being repaired and resold. My wife, Joanne, loves to watch such programs, which inspire her to dream up little projects to make our home more beautiful. Countless numbers of YouTube videos of the "how-to" variety allow us to view repairs taking place step-by-step. In his stand-up routine, comedian Jerry Seinfeld observed that men, especially, are drawn like zombies to watching other men repairing something in their driveway or on their house!

There is something innately pleasing about watching someone masterfully repair something. I know that I stand in awe and amazement of my best friend, Joe, who can fix just about anything. He has repaired everything from my toilet, ceiling fan, and sewer pipes to my thermostat, refrigerator door, and teeth (yes, he is my dentist).

Successfully repairing things or watching others repair things gives us pleasure. It is interesting to note that when the COVID-19 pandemic forced the world into isolation, many of us responded by undertaking home repairs! When something is successfully repaired, it feels as though order has been restored to the entire universe. Perhaps because, in some way, that's exactly what occurs: thanks to repairs, things go back to the way they "should be." And this, I believe, is one of God's most attractive qualities: God repairs things.

Throughout the Old Testament, God seeks to repair the relationship that his Chosen People have damaged. Throughout the New Testament, Jesus performs countless miracles that "restore" things: he restores health (healing mind, body, and spirit); he restores sustenance (changing water into wine, the multiplication of the loaves and fish); he restores the natural order (calming of the sea); and he restores life (raising people from the dead). It's no wonder he attracted crowds. On our journey to become fully human, we would do well to learn from God and his only Son, Jesus Christ, a.k.a. the "Divine Physician," who repairs and restores us when we are damaged by sin.

What was the last thing you successfully repaired? How did it make you feel?

_____

_____

_____

God to the Rescue

God creates—and God restores. In Scripture, we see God establish a sacred covenant with his people and then continually work to restore, rescue, mend, repair, heal, strengthen, redeem, renew, and reconcile (words that, combined, appear more than six hundred times in Scripture) on behalf of his people. The preeminent example of God rescuing and restoring his people is the Exodus story as God, through Moses, leads his people out of slavery in Egypt to freedom in the Promised Land. There, he establishes them as a people. While it would be nice to say that they all lived happily ever after, that was unfortunately not the case, as the people of Israel continually strayed from God's love. And how did God respond each time? By being the "adult in the room" and taking the initiative to restore and reconcile.

Think for a moment about rescuers you see on the news: first responders who place themselves in danger as they dramatically run toward and reach out to grasp the hands of those in danger and lead them to safety. Rescuers take risks. God continually takes the risk of rescuing his people no matter what danger they find themselves in.

Recall a recent news story of a first responder rescuing someone. Think about the situation and the mindset of the rescuer. What qualities do first responders need to possess?

_____

_____

_____

It is no surprise that the Old Testament is replete with rescue stories spanning many centuries—stories in which God rescues people from danger and restores them to safety and security. And, while the Exodus event forms the first "bookend," so to speak, of the rescue epic we know as the Old Testament, the other "bookend" would be the Exile event. After many centuries of independence, the kingdom of Israel, because of losing faith in God, was destroyed and the people were carried off into exile in Babylon. There, the Jewish people wondered if the kingdom would ever be restored and if they would ever be reconciled with their God. God's answer was, of course, to respond with mercy. There, during the experience of exile, God said the following through the prophet Ezekiel:

> I will gather you from the nations and bring you back from the countries where you have been scattered, and I will give you back the land of Israel again. They will return to it and remove all its vile images and detestable idols. I will give them an undivided heart and put a new spirit in them; I will remove from them their heart of stone and give them a heart of flesh. Then they will follow my decrees and be careful to keep my laws. They will be my people, and I will be their God. (Ezekiel 11:17–20)

For Christians, this promise was fulfilled in the coming of God's only Son, Jesus Christ, our Redeemer (reconciler).

Describe an experience in which God rescued, restored, or repaired you.

_____

_____

Christmas Is about God's Ultimate Repair Job

It is interesting to note that in the first verse of one of the most cherished and famous Christmas carols, "Hark! The Herald Angels Sing," we proclaim the newborn king as a reconciler—the One who has come to repair our relationship with God:

> Hark! The herald angels sing,
> "Glory to the newborn King:
> Peace on earth and mercy mild,
> God and sinners reconciled!"

The heralding angels mince no words in describing the effect of this birth: the repairing and reconciling of our relationship with God. And, as always, it is accomplished through God's initiative.

In many other Christmas carols, we sing of "peace on earth." Unfortunately, however, we tend to think that this refers solely to the cessation of wars. And while that is true, peace on earth occurs whenever we experience God's generous mercy, are reconciled with God, and align our wills with the will of God. When our relationship with God is repaired and we are aligned with his will, we call this righteousness or justification.

Like his heavenly Father, Jesus' foster father, Joseph, specialized in creating and repairing things as a carpenter. Joseph, in turn, taught Jesus his trade. It is no surprise, then, that when Jesus grew up, he got to work doing exactly what his Father sent him to do: repairing relationships and reconciling people to the Father. And so, we celebrate this child-king because, in him, our relationship with the Father is repaired.

> **How can Christmas—the Incarnation—be a "reconciliation" event in your life?**
>
> _____
>
> _____
>
> _____

See, I Make All Things New!

Ultimately, God's promise is to repair everything! The book of Revelation, which so many people incorrectly use to predict when the world will end, is really about how God will repair the world. As the book reaches its climax, John's vision talks about "a new heaven and a new earth, for the first heaven and the first earth had passed away" (Revelation 21:1). Next, in a very dramatic scene, a loud voice from one seated on a throne (the risen Christ) proclaims, "I am making everything new!" (Revelation 21:5). And while this is put forward as the "ultimate" end of God's plan, we do not have to wait until the end of the world for this to happen. Saint Paul says very clearly that "if anyone is in Christ, he is a new creation; the old has gone, the new has come!" (2 Corinthians 5:17). The overriding benefit of following Jesus (being "in Christ") is that we are made new: we are "repaired."

In his book *Simply Christian*, Bible scholar and Anglican bishop N.T. Wright tells us that God's intention is not to abandon this world in favor of heaven but rather to "remake it." He emphasizes that the goal of discipleship is not to "get to heaven when you die" but rather to enjoy "a new bodily life within God's new world." Scripture does not promise us that God will "abandon ship" and take righteous people to heaven but rather that those who live "in Christ" will enjoy a new heaven *and* a new earth. God is not so much into "demo" as he is into "reno." And, while this restoration project will not reach completion until the end of time, Jesus' birth, life, death, and resurrection have initiated the final phase of the project. Jesus invites us to participate in the ongoing advancement of the kingdom of God, which exists wherever God's will reigns.

> **What does it mean to you that "the goal of Christianity is not to 'get to heaven when you die'" but rather to enjoy "a new bodily life within God's new world"? Is this a completely different perspective than you were raised with? How so?**

Fixing for a Living

One of the ways that the Holy Spirit invites us to share in divine energy is by prompting us to fix things (which goes against the grain of a "throw-away" or "disposable" culture). In fact, many people choose careers that primarily focus on doing just that—fixing things . . .

doctors	construction workers
dentists	plumbers
nurses	painters
lawyers	therapists

auto mechanics

software developers

electricians

HVAC technicians

landscapers

roofers

those who repair shoes

tailors

maintenance engineers

interior designers

those who repair clocks and
  watches

. . . .and so on. Not only is there something innately pleasing about successfully repairing something, there is also something innately divine! Repairs bring us closer to the way things should be: the way God intended them to be. If your full-time job involves repairing things, be sure to remind yourself that you are imitating God, and find affirmation in doing work that so closely emulates what God does full-time as well. If repairing things is not your full-time work, find ways to engage in side jobs, activities, or hobbies that enable you to repair things, as a way of inviting the Holy Spirit to renew the divine energy within you. Consider the following:

home improvements

woodworking

restoring furniture/antiques

reupholstering furniture

refinishing floors

sewing

gardening

landscaping

restoring automobiles

bicycle repair

welding/soldering

sharpening knives

bookbinding

jewelry repair

computer repair

editing (text or video)

electrical repair

plumbing repair

guitar repair

In what ways does your career involve making repairs? What hobbies, side jobs, or activities involve you in repairing things?

_____

_____

_____

Repairing Lives

When we engage in fixing/repairing things, we are doing it for someone who will benefit from such repairs, either someone else or ourselves. By repairing something for someone else, we are, in some small (or large) way, repairing their lives. Sometimes, however, we need to do much more than repair items or objects that belong to another person; we may need to help repair lives that are broken. Many people's lives are broken because of unemployment, sickness, homelessness, abuse, incarceration, mental health issues, substance abuse, loss of loved ones, injury, broken relationships, and so on. In response to this brokenness, we are called to emulate God and to initiate repairs.

In the Christian tradition, these repairs are called Works of Mercy. Through the Corporal Works of Mercy, we seek to repair the physical brokenness of people's lives. We do this by

- feeding those who are hungry
- giving drink to those who are thirsty
- sheltering those who have been made homeless
- visiting and caring for those who are sick

- visiting those who are imprisoned
- burying the dead
- giving alms to those made poor

Through the Spiritual Works of Mercy, we seek to repair the spiritual brokenness of people's lives. We do this by

- counseling those in doubt and despair
- instructing those who do not yet know the joy of the gospel
- admonishing those whose actions are hurting others
- comforting those who are in sorrow
- forgiving those who have hurt us
- bearing wrongs patiently
- praying for the living and the dead

We should also note how closely the divine attribute of restoration is tied to the divine attribute of compassion, which we discussed in chapter 5. Authentic compassion requires us to truly listen and observe because often we need only to accompany someone without trying to "fix" them, trusting that God will bring about restoration.

> **To what extent do you practice the Corporal and Spiritual Works of Mercy? Name one person toward whom you will extend mercy. What will you do for them?**
>
> _____
>
> _____
>
> _____

Repairing Structures That Harm People

It's one thing to repair a crack in the wall of a house. It's another thing to repair the foundation of a house that is settling and causing cracks in the walls. The Works of Mercy can be compared to fixing the crack in the wall. Social justice can be compared to repairing the foundation, the root of the problem. Participating in social justice—bringing about major repairs to the structures of our society that are causing harm in people's lives—is one of the ways that we emulate God, whose most significant saving act in the Old Testament was one of social justice: bringing about an end to the economic system in Egypt that was built on the backs of enslaved Jewish people.

Today, many societal structures continue to benefit some people at the expense of others. Racism, sexual discrimination, human trafficking, political corruption, and human rights abuses are just a few examples of injustices that continue to plague our nation and our world. God loathes injustice and raises up people like Moses in every age to call for major repairs to our societal structures. If you want to tap into divine energy, get involved in social justice activities (such as the Catholic Campaign for Human Development, Habitat for Humanity, Heifer International, Oxfam, or Catholic Relief Services) and help God repair the world!

What societal injustices concern you the most and what might you do to help repair them?

_____

_____

_____

Repairing Relationships: Someone Has to Be the Adult in the Room

Up to now, most of the suggestions we've looked at for resembling God and living the divine attributes sound pretty inviting and perhaps even fun. However, the characteristic that we are dealing with here—repairing relationships—does not come easily to many of us. It is not easy to be a reconciler; in fact, it's hard work.

When my wife and I occasionally have a spat, we typically go off into our separate corners to stew in anger and think of all the ways we can come out on top this time. Then, the waiting game begins: who will be the "adult in the room" and make the first move toward reconciling?

When it comes to our relationship with God, there is no doubt who the adult in the room is! God always takes the initiative to reconcile our relationship with him—even though we alone are the transgressors! It is good to know that God's default setting is to reconcile—to bring us back to his loving embrace whenever we stray.

Describe a time when you were compelled to be the adult in the room by initiating reconciliation. How did the experience go?

_____

_____

_____

Throughout human history, many religions and acts of worship have been centered around appeasing an angry god by offering sacrifices, as if paying a debt. For a time, our Jewish ancestors thought they needed to do the same thing. God, however, wanted nothing to do with it: "For I desire mercy, not sacrifice, and acknowledgment of God rather than burnt offerings" (Hosea 6:6).

By the way, *this* is why Jesus cleansed the temple: his primary concern wasn't that there was money changing going on in the area around the temple where people bought lambs and doves to sacrifice. Rather, he was making a powerful statement that this kind of worship was to cease. The God of mercy did not need to be appeased by animal sacrifices. He just wanted hearts that were reconciled and merciful.

To Be Human Is to Need Repair

One of the most glorious feasts of the liturgical year is Pentecost, the day on which we joyfully ask God to send forth his Spirit and RENEW the face of the earth (responsorial psalm)! Too often, this feast is trivialized as the "birthday of the church." While this is well intentioned and in some sense truthful, it misses the bigger point of Pentecost: it is the celebration of restoration—a restoration made possible by the infusion of the Holy Spirit in the hearts of those who follow and proclaim Jesus' way of living. It is the restoration or repair of the scattering that occurred in the story of the Tower of Babel (Genesis 11:1–9).

What the crowds saw on Pentecost was a group of people with restored lives, proclaiming that it was through Jesus Christ—God in the flesh—that they found restoration. The men who had abandoned and denied Jesus at the time of his suffering and death and then hid in fear were now restored. And they now invited others to share in this restoration.

We human beings have a perpetual need for renewal and restoration. To be human is, in essence, to be "broken" (we are not perfect) and in need of repair. People in Twelve Step programs learn this difficult truth as the first step toward sobriety/healing. We often fool ourselves into thinking that we can be "purified" by being members of a church when, the truth is, the best we can do (and something we *need* to do) is to be in recovery. It is through the Spirit of God that we find such recovery and renewal. And we enter more deeply into the life of the Spirit and a life of discipleship by engaging in various forms of repairing and restoring the world around us—just as God is doing every day. When we recognize our brokenness, we acknowledge that we are still a work in progress; we are on our way to becoming fully human.

Ultimately, repairing things restores hope. As I write these lines, people living on the Gulf Coast are awaiting repairs to the power grid that will restore electricity after yet another hurricane. Countless friends, on social media, have been expressing gratefulness for repairs as their lights, air conditioning, and refrigerators are restored, and, in the same breath, are encouraging hope for others who still await the much-needed repairs.

In a similar way, when we find our minds and hearts restored by the mercy and compassion of God's healing (repairing) love, we become grateful and seek to extend that hope to others who need restoration. Repairing relationships after times of conflict can often bring about closer, stronger relationships. Discipleship is all about being repaired and inviting others to be repaired, not through our own power but through the power of God, whose Spirit renews the face of the earth.

I daresay that the most accurate litmus test to determine if someone is filled with the Holy Spirit is whether they are consumed with and actively involved in repairing lives . . . because that's what God does.

When has someone extended hope to you and helped "restore" you?

_____

_____

_____

Blessed Are Those Who Repair Relationships

In the Beatitudes, Jesus proclaims, "Blessed are the peacemakers!" That line could easily be paraphrased in the following manner: "Blessed are those who repair relationships!" Such relationships can be between nations and organizations, or they can simply be between friends and family members. To be a peacemaker is to be someone who repairs broken relationships. By participating in this "ministry of reconciliation" (2 Corinthians 5:18), we partner with God in ordering creation toward its ultimate goal: the fulfillment of the kingdom of God. Here are some important points to keep in mind when it comes to peacemaking or restoring relationships. Conflicts . . .

- typically involve an inability to recognize and respond to the things that matter to the other person. To be a peacemaker, one needs to practice empathy or have the ability to see from (the other person's viewpoint) and to respect differences.
- often involve strong, explosive, angry, hurtful, and resentful reactions. To be a peacemaker, one needs to remain calm and rely on nondefensive and respectful reactions.

- often result in the withdrawal of love and a growing separation from one another. To be a peacemaker, one must have a willingness to forgive and to move past the conflict without holding onto resentments.

- typically involve an inability to compromise and a desire to punish the other. To be a peacemaker, one must be open to compromise and interested in a positive outcome.

- leave us feeling fearful of encountering the other person. To be a peacemaker, one must believe that facing conflict head on is the best thing for all involved.

- are usually driven by ego. To be a peacemaker, one needs to set aside the ego.

- can develop instantly and may fester for long periods of time. To be a peacemaker, one needs to recognize that reconciliation is a process that will take time and cannot be rushed.

- often result in a loss of trust. To be a peacemaker is to risk trusting the other.

- leave one or both parties feeling threatened. To be a peacemaker, one needs to assure the other party/parties involved that they are safe and that you pose no threat to them.

- can be paralyzing, can stunt growth and progress, and can end relationships. To be a peacemaker, one must see conflicts as opportunities for a relationship to grow and for trust to be reestablished.

- tend to focus on the past. To be a peacemaker is to focus on the future.

- involve holding on. To be a peacemaker is to be willing to let go.

When were you called on to be a peacemaker in a relationship? What strategies did you employ? What lessons did you learn from that attempt to be a peacemaker?

_____

_____

_____

In Summary . . .

God seeks to mend, heal, rescue, repair, and restore. When we engage in repairs or benefit from someone making repairs for us, it feels as though things are put right. As human beings, we need restoration because we are incapable of overcoming sin's power without God's help. We can become more fully human and tap into divine energy by embracing this divine attribute as we immerse ourselves in repairing things and, especially, in repairing relationships.

Scripture Passages That Reveal/ Emphasize God's Desire to Repair/Restore

Then the Lord your God will restore your fortunes and have compassion on you and gather you again from all the nations where he scattered you.

Deuteronomy 30:3

Restore us, O God;
> make your face shine on us,
> that we may be saved.

Psalm 80:3

But those who hope in the L ORD
  will renew their strength.
They will soar on wings like eagles;
  they will run and not grow weary,
  they will walk and not be faint.
Isaiah 40:31

I will bring my people Israel back from exile.
  They will rebuild the ruined cities and live in them.
They will plant vineyards and drink their wine;
  they will make gardens and eat their fruit.
Amos 9:14

Then he said to the man, "Stretch out your hand." So he stretched
it out and it was completely restored, just as sound as the other.
Matthew 12:13

Then I saw a new heaven and a new earth, for the first heaven and
the first earth had passed away, and there was no longer any sea.
Revelation 21:1

**Which of the above Scripture quotes speaks to you most
strongly about God's desire/power to restore? Why?**

_____

_____

_____

As you reflect on this chapter, what is one shift you can make in your life to tap into the divine energy of restoration and repair?

_____

_____

_____

Chapter 7

Share Generously and Selflessly

The heart that gives, gathers.
—Tao Te Ching

I'm Feeling Generous

According to Buddhist wisdom, if you wish to be unhappy, think about yourself. If you wish to be happy, think about others. When we experience unhappiness, our focus turns inward upon ourselves. While it's good to tend to the causes of our unhappiness and do our inner work, one of the ways out of the unhappiness we feel is to shift our attention outward toward others. Which brings us to the topic of generosity, essentially "prosocial behavior" or acts that benefit others.

We tend to think of generosity as an occasional act of kindness expressed monetarily: we send a check to a charity, drop an envelope in the church basket, purchase Girl Scout cookies, put some money in the Salvation Army kettle, and so on. These are generous acts that tend to make us feel better about ourselves. Generosity, however, is much more than an action, and it does not always involve money. It is not a feeling that comes and goes. True generosity is a permanent disposition: an attitude and a way of proceeding. Generosity originates in the heart. It is not an occasional action, feeling, or whim: it is an orientation toward life.

> **Who do you know personally who has a "generous heart"? What does it mean to say that generosity is an orientation toward life?**
>
> _____
>
> _____
>
> _____

God Is Generosity

According to Scripture, God's generosity is not occasional, nor is it simply an attribute or characteristic of God. Rather, generosity is who God is. God's very essence is to give Godself to others. God is not merely generous; God IS generosity (in much the same way that we say "God is love").

God's first act according to the Genesis story was to generously create the cosmos and share it with his children. The book of Revelation reveals God generously re-creating heaven and earth at the end of time. Sandwiched between those two amazingly generous divine actions, we find story after story of God generously sharing love, mercy, and compassion with people, culminating in the generous sharing of his only Son, Jesus, with humankind. Scripture reveals generosity as integral to the "divine economy"—the process or system by which God "distributes" his abundance among his people. When we are generous, we are simply sharing in this divine economy. For a life of authentic discipleship, we are called to reorient our lives to be less about ourselves and more about others. God's divine economy calls us to an attitude of abundance rather than of scarcity (more on this later). We are called to have a disposition of generosity: an approach to life that seeks to share with others. In essence, generosity is not so much about what we do but rather about who we are.

In what ways has God been generous to you?

_____

_____

_____

How Noble of You

The word _generous_ can be traced to the Latin word _generosus_, which means "noble birth." We know from history that it was the responsibility of those in the noble class to see to the needs of those less well off. In fact, the French term _noblesse oblige_ translates to "nobility obligates," which means simply that those who have great wealth have a responsibility to share with those less fortunate. For nobility, being generous was to be their role in society. The biblical notion of generosity takes this to the extreme, especially in the New Testament, where the baptized are seen as sharing in Jesus' ministry as priest, prophet, and _king_. This means that we share in the nobility of Christ the King and thus have a responsibility to be generous to others as he is to us.

The word *noble* means a variety of things, not the least of which are "preeminent," "highly virtuous," and "deserving respect." To be generous is a preeminent requirement of those who identify as disciples of Christ, and thus, it is noble. To be generous is highly virtuous, and thus, it is noble. To be generous is deserving of respect, and thus, it is noble. In Buddhism, the Four Noble Truths are considered the essential truths of life that lead to liberation from suffering. This means that being generous—a noble act—sets us free!

> **How do/can you share in the "nobility of Christ"? How is this notion of nobility related to generosity?**
>
> _____
>
> _____
>
> _____

Paying It Forward: Generosity as a Contagion

We use the phrase "paying it forward" to describe the act of showing kindness and generosity to others as a way of "repaying" a kindness we received from someone else. The following story illustrates this. The great German composer Johannes Brahms was informed that an admirer of his had left him a substantial amount of money (1,000 pounds) in his will. Brahms, who was deeply moved by this act of generosity, wrote to a friend describing the touching act. He went on to explain to his friend, however, that since he did not really need the money, he was enjoying it in a "most agreeable manner": redistributing it to others!

The virtuous and generous action of the individual who left this large sum of money to Brahms inspired him to imitate the action for the benefit of others. In fact, research reveals that generosity does indeed spread from one to another like a contagion. A study conducted in 2010 shows that, of participants invited to contribute money to others, those who were the beneficiaries of generosity were three times more likely to contribute than those who had not received generosity. Likewise, a study conducted in 2016 reveals that participants were more moved to donate simply by watching others make generous donations. Now there's a contagion we don't want to contain!

When was a time that you felt compelled to "pay it forward"? When was a time you benefited from someone else "paying it forward"?

_____

_____

_____

New Math

Biblical generosity introduces us to a sort of "new math." Typically, our education in mathematics leads us to conclude that if you have a few things and you give some of those things away, you will have fewer things. Biblical generosity, however, insists on a very different answer to the same equation. Scripture teaches us a "new math" that says: if you have a few things and you give some of those things to others who need them, you will have more. Somehow, when it comes to generosity, when you subtract, the sum grows larger.

It's quite difficult for us, however, to let go of the old math. One of the reasons for that is that our culture tends to promote a "scarcity mentality" rather than an "abundance mentality"—terms coined by the late Stephen Covey in his book *The 7 Habits of Highly Effective People*. According to Covey, scarcity mentality can be thought of as picturing life as a pie that can be sliced up only so many ways before it's all gone. Thus, if some people take bigger pieces, that means everyone else will have less. This scarcity mentality is especially prevalent in the corporate world and in capitalism per se. Think of how many ads create a sense of urgency by telling us that we need to "buy now" or forever miss this once-in-a-lifetime opportunity.

The late Dr. Wayne Dyer (psychotherapist, lecturer, and author) often explained that to have a scarcity mentality means to evaluate our life in terms of its lacks. He said that if we dwell on scarcity, we are putting our energy into what we do not have, and this continues to be our life experience. A person with an abundance mentality, on the other hand, believes that there is enough to go around; there is an endless universe to work in, and we are part of that endless universe.

What are the dangers of dwelling on scarcity? Do you tend toward an abundance mentality or a scarcity mentality? Who do you know who has an "abundance mentality," and how can you emulate him or her?

_____

_____

The Makings of a Banquet

A great example of these two mentalities clashing can be found in the story of Jesus feeding the five thousand, which appears in all four Gospels. Upon realizing that the crowds were hungry, Jesus asked his disciples to take inventory of what food they had. That quick inventory revealed a supply of five loaves and two fish. What kind of a meal can you make out of five loaves and two fish? The answer depends upon your perspective. The disciples clearly thought that five loaves and two fish were not enough.

To Jesus, however, it sounded like the beginning of a feast. Does this mean that Jesus was out of touch with reality? Anyone with common sense can see that 5 + 2 does not equal 5,000. Jesus, however, is in fact quite sane. He just has an abundance mentality. Jesus is not out of touch with reality but sees reality as full of possibilities. Like the disciples, Jesus saw a meager amount of food: five loaves and two fish. Unlike the disciples, however, Jesus had imagination enough to see the banquet these bits could become.

And let's not forget: there were twelve baskets of *leftovers* when everyone had had their fill! It is this kind of mentality that makes generosity possible, and it is how we are called to live today: to see infinite possibilities and to extend generosity to all we meet.

When have you witnessed someone "create a banquet" with limited resources? When have you seen someone take a bad situation and creatively turn it into a success?

_____

_____

That's a Lot of Wine!

Perhaps one of the most striking images of God's generosity and banquet mentality can be found in the story of Jesus' first miracle at the wedding at Cana (John 2:1–11). As you recall, Jesus, his mother, and his disciples are attending a wedding feast in Cana when the bride and groom run out of wine. Jesus' mother, Mary, nudges him to do something to remedy the situation and, being the obedient son he is, Jesus does just that: he instructs the servants to fill six stone jars with water and then to draw some out to take to the head waiter. Somewhere along the way, Jesus turns that water into the finest wine. Now, that is miraculous enough! However, it is striking that the story tells us that each of the six stone jars holds 20 to 30 gallons. If my math is correct, that's between 120 and 180 gallons, or the equivalent of over 900 bottles of wine!

That's a lot of wine!

The point of this story is that, in God's kingdom—which is often depicted in Scripture as a banquet—there is an abundance of goodness! There is, indeed, enough to go around, several times. God's kingdom is marked by extravagance and abundance, and through Jesus Christ, this kingdom has burst into our midst. We are called to share generously this abundance with everyone.

In what ways has God's generosity been "overflowing" in your life?

_____

_____

_____

You Don't Have to Be Rich to Be Generous

To have a generous heart does not mean that you have money to throw around. It means that your focus is on the needs of others. Some of the most generous people in the world live below the poverty level. To have a generous heart means to have a disposition—a lifestyle—of generosity that permeates every area of life. And the first step in cultivating this disposition is to recognize and be appreciative for what one has instead of focusing on what one lacks or wants. As cliché as this may sound, it means developing an attitude of gratitude.

Giving to others is almost effortless when we recognize all that we have received. A generous heart gives, not out of a sense of duty, guilt, or a desire to show off, but out of appreciation for what one has and out of compassion for others who may lack what they need. True generosity comes from the heart. The heart, of course, is a muscle, and we know that muscles need to be exercised. In the same way, a generous heart becomes stronger the more we engage in acts of generosity or the giving of good things to others. These good things do not necessarily have to be money. Here is just a sampling of the many ways we can be generous, even if we have little or no money or material possessions to share. As you read through this list, take note of how these ways of being generous are consistent with the other divine attributes we've looked at throughout this book.

We can be generous with our

- thoughts: giving people the benefit of the doubt, trusting that they have the best intentions
- words: speaking words of positivity, encouragement, courtesy, and compassion
- possessions: sharing what we have with others
- time: volunteering, giving people attention, spending quality time with others, coming to the assistance of others

- influence: sharing connections and relationships that can help another
- hospitality: making people feel at home, welcoming people into our home
- life: giving blood and becoming an organ donor
- listening: truly paying attention to people
- physical health/strength: helping others with physical tasks
- knowledge: helping others to learn and acquire knowledge and skills
- forgiveness: letting go of grudges and striving for reconciliation
- talents and expertise: using our gifts to assist others who don't have that gift
- creativity: using imagination and creativity to engage, entertain, and assist others
- food: cooking and sharing meals and recipes with others, taking others out to eat
- prayers: praying for those in need and praying for our enemies
- hope and joy: lifting others out of despair

Which of the above are you most generous with? In which area(s) do you wish to be more generous?

_____

_____

_____

Stewardship: Giving of Our Time, Talent, and Treasure

In the Nicene Creed, we proclaim our belief and our trust in God as the Creator of "all things." In this creed, we are expressing our belief that everything we have is a generous gift from God. Our response is to live as caretakers or "stewards" of God's gifts, using them wisely and sharing them generously for the good of all. Stewardship, then, is not a parish program, nor is it ultimately about money. It is an attitude and a way of life. Stewardship is a lifestyle that enhances our relationships with God and our brothers and sisters by calling us to center our lives on Jesus rather than on ourselves.

- We do so by sharing our time with others, realizing that we are all living on "borrowed time."

- We do so by sharing our talents in service of others, knowing that our talents are gifts from God.

- We do so by sharing our material possessions, acknowledging that the resources of the earth were created by God for the good of all people.

Stewardship and, ultimately, generosity, is not about giving up a portion of what is ours. Rather, it is a matter of recognizing that everything we have comes from God and we are called to generously share a portion of that abundance with others. And, after doing so, to be grateful for what we are blessed to keep for ourselves.

> **In what ways are you generous with your time? Talent? Treasure? How can you be more generous in each area?**
>
> _____
>
> _____
>
> _____

Generosity and Selflessness: Laying Down Our Lives

Generosity is antithetical to selfishness or self-centeredness. By its very nature, generosity is selfless and other-centered. No doubt, this is why the Gospel verse of John 3:16 is one of the most widely quoted Bible verses. It describes the essence of God's generous and selfless love: "For God so loved the world that he gave his one and only Son, that whoever believes in him shall not perish but have eternal life." Jesus, in turn, proclaimed this selfless love: "Greater love has no one than this, that he lay down his life for his friends" (John 15:13)—words he embodied by dying on the cross.

Over the centuries of church history, many men and women have laid down their lives for their faith (we call them martyrs). Many military personnel as well as first responders have laid down their lives for others. What about the rest of us? Is the "greatest love" out of reach for the average person because we have not and probably will not physically die/be killed because of our faith? I think we have too narrowly defined what it means to "lay down your life" for others. While some, like Jesus, actually die for others, the rest of us are called to generously lay down our lives for others each and every day. To die for others is the ultimate example, but to lay down your life means to set your own needs aside to tend to the needs of others.

We are called to do this every day. Parents and spouses set aside their own needs to tend to the needs of their children and one another. Teachers and catechists set aside their own needs to tend to the needs of their students. Doctors and nurses set aside their own needs to tend to the needs of their patients. Many adults set aside their own needs to care for elderly parents. Workers set aside their own needs to tend to the needs of their customers or coworkers. And so on. In essence, to "lay down your life" means to be generous. Jesus says that this is the greatest love.

> **Who has generously "laid down their life" for you? In what ways have you/are you laying down your life for someone else?**
>
> _____
>
> _____
>
> _____

God's Generosity is NOT to Be Measured by Our Monetary/Material Success

One unfortunate misrepresentation of the Christian message is the notion that God's generosity is manifested in our monetary and/or material success. As I mentioned earlier, some segments of Christianity have adopted what is now known as the "prosperity gospel"—the notion that by placing your faith in Jesus, praying for his generous blessings, and donating generously to your church, you will be rewarded with material and financial success and "earn" your way into heaven. Such material success is often flaunted by the proponents and preachers of the prosperity gospel: flashily dressed televangelists with private jets, yachts, and multimillion-dollar mansions.

As a result of relentless preaching of the prosperity gospel, estimates are that nearly a third of American Christians believe that if you give your money to God, God will reward you with more money. Prosperity is seen as divine blessing and reward. In contrast to the preaching of the prosperity gospel, Pope Francis regularly promotes the idea of a "poor church," telling an audience shortly after becoming pope, "How I would like a church that is poor and for the poor." Speaking on the World Day of the Poor (November 17, 2019), Pope Francis said, "You who are small, you who are poor, you who are fragile, you are the treasure of the Church."

This notion of the poor as the "treasure of the Church" can be traced to St. Lawrence, a deacon during the third century when the Church in Rome was being persecuted by Emperor Valerian, who sought to confiscate any and all of the Church's treasures. Lawrence, who was given the responsibility of protecting the Church's treasures by Pope Sixtus II, began selling off the treasures and distributing the money to those who were poor. The emperor had Pope Sixtus killed and set his sights on Lawrence, giving him three days to round up and hand over the Church's treasures before having him killed.

Lawrence promptly assembled a group of people who were poor, sick, and vulnerable and presented them to the emperor as the "Church's treasures." The emperor was not amused, and Lawrence was promptly executed, but not before he had proclaimed the true gospel: God's generosity is not to be measured by material wealth. Nor is it a "tit for tat" arrangement. God's desire is for ALL his children to enjoy the generous abundance of creation. Remember, wealth per se is not evil. It is just dangerous. And generosity is the antidote.

> **What can you learn from those who are poor? How can those who are poor be thought of as the "treasure of the Church"? How can generosity be the antidote for the dangers of riches in your life?**
>
> _____
>
> _____
>
> _____

In Summary . . .

God seeks to share Godself with us. In the Christian tradition, the climax of this self-sharing was the sending of his only Son, Jesus, to become one of us. Generosity—the selfless sharing with others, especially with those in need—is more than a feeling; it is a disposition and a noble way of proceeding in life. We can become more fully human and tap into divine energy by selflessly sharing our time, talent, and treasure with others.

Scripture Passages That Reveal/Emphasize God's Generosity and Our Call to Be Generous

A generous man will himself be blessed,
  for he shares his food with the poor.
Proverbs 22:9

Do not store up for yourselves treasures on earth, where moth and rust destroy, and where thieves break in and steal. But store up for yourselves treasures in heaven, where moth and rust do not destroy and where thieves do not break in and steal. For where your treasure is, there your heart will be also.
Matthew 6:19–21

For God so loved the world that he gave his one and only Son, that whoever believes in him shall not perish but have eternal life.
John 3:16

In everything I did, I showed you that by this kind of hard work we must help the weak, remembering the words the Lord Jesus himself said: "It is more blessed to give than to receive."
Acts 20:35

Each man should give what he has decided in his heart to give, not reluctantly or under compulsion, for God loves a cheerful giver.
2 Corinthians 9:7

And do not forget to do good and to share with others, for with such sacrifices God is pleased.
Hebrews 13:16

Which of the above Scripture quotes speaks to you most strongly about God's generosity and our call to be generous to one another? Why?

_____

_____

As you reflect on this chapter, what is one shift you can make in your life to tap into the divine energy of generosity and selflessness?

_____

_____

_____

Chapter 8

Be Still

Everything that's created comes out of silence. Your thoughts emerge
from the nothingness of silence. Your words come out of this void.
Your very essence emerged from emptiness. All creativity
requires some stillness.

—Wayne Dyer

Be Still? I Thought You Wanted Us to "Get Up!"

I began this book with the story of Elijah and the command from
the angel to "get up!" It may seem odd and downright contradictory
to end this book by telling you now to "be still!" I assure you, however, that I consciously chose to wrap up this book by talking about
the need for all of us to occasionally "be still" precisely because it is a
necessary part of spiritual renewal. Even Elijah was allowed to sleep a
while longer before the angel nudged him a second time, telling him
to "get up!"

Think of it this way. Have you ever come across a spiritual tradition that has NOT involved stillness as a means to well-being?

I didn't think so. In fact, Christianity maintains that our salvation
entered the world on a "Silent Night."

Any spiritual tradition that you can think of will identify stillness (solitude, silence, etc.) as a fundamental principle for attaining spiritual growth. In fact, this notion of experiencing intentional stillness is so critical in the Judeo-Christian tradition that it is named as one of the Ten Commandments: You shall keep holy the Sabbath day.

How often do you find time to be still? What do you do to quiet yourself?

_____

_____

_____

Observing Sabbath

Doing exercises helps our muscles grow. The interesting thing, however, is that muscles do not grow while we're exercising but afterward when we're resting. Doing exercise causes small fibers in our muscles to tear. When we are at rest, the muscle fibers repair themselves and grow. That's how muscles get bigger. It is resting that helps them grow.

In a similar way, the third commandment teaches us that the only way we will grow spiritually is by taking a day of rest from our normal routine. To keep holy the Sabbath day is to set aside one day a week—Sunday for Christians—to rest and to worship (realign ourselves with) God. This day of resting in God's presence allows us to grow spiritually.

This is important to know because we live in a culture that tends to emphasize DOING as the most important measure of one's overall value. Even advertisements for vacations and cruises emphasize all the activities we can do while we're there. While it is important for us to be productive, we must recognize that our productivity is not limitless. Like a battery that needs to be recharged, we need to plug into divine energy for renewal. We do this by observing the third commandment. Isn't it awesome that one of the Ten Commandments, in effect says, "You shall take a day off"?

> **Do you value times of stillness, or do you see them as a waste of time? How much emphasis do you place on productivity?**
>
> _____
>
> _____
>
> _____

Sabbath as Re-Alignment

The word for worship (in Hebrew) means to "bow down to." Notice what we do when we bow: we physically align ourselves—we orient ourselves—with the person or thing to which we are bowing. To bow to someone or something is to say, in essence, "I direct all of my being to you." This is why the first commandment directs us not to bow down before any false gods but rather to direct our entire being to God alone. As disciples of Christ, the way we strive to keep ourselves aligned with God is through worship. The third commandment—keep holy the Sabbath day—is designed as a day for realignment.

Without worship we can easily veer off path, often unknowingly sliding into patterns of life that take us away from loving God and neighbor and, instead, keep us focused on ourselves. In a sense, we all suffer from a type of spiritual amnesia. It is human nature to forget to pay attention to our spiritual dimension. For disciples of Christ, worship is our constant reminder that our lives need realignment to be directed toward God, who is love. In essence, to worship is to love, for to love is to direct all our attention—our very being—to the presence of another.

Every so often, our cars need a wheel alignment. In the same way, the third commandment is an invitation for us to get an alignment for our souls. We do this by setting aside a day to be still—to pause from our doing and focus our attention on being.

> **When was a time you felt a need to "realign" yourself with God? What did you do to make this realignment happen?**
>
> _____
>
> _____
>
> _____

Signs That You Need to Pause

When we fail to "be still" or to pause for Sabbath rest, we run the risk of becoming "human doings" instead of "human beings." This point is crucial because we are people created in the image and likeness of God. Recall that God revealed himself to Moses as the great "I AM." When Moses asked God for his name—his central identity—God did not respond "I Do" but rather "I AM." To take this even a step further, it is important to note, as I explain in my book *A Well-Built Faith*, God is not a "supreme being." A supreme being is a being that is simply superior to other beings. God is the Creator of human beings. God is not a being: God is the ground of being—the very essence of being. God just is. The Holy Spirit invites us to tap into divine energy by prompting us to take time to just "be." No doubt this is why God famously said, "Be still, and know that I am God" (Psalm 46:10).

In his book *The Power of Pause*, author, humorist, and inspirational speaker Terry Hershey offers some telltale signs that we need to focus on being instead of doing.

- We find ourselves adding more to our to-do lists, even though we already feel overwhelmed.
- We often wish we had an extra day in our week.
- We have been rewarded for working to the point of exhaustion.
- We find that our weekends are just as jam-packed as our workdays.
- Taking time to relax every day is seldom a priority.
- We often feel stressed out and overtired.
- We have tried to pray, only to find our mind swimming with tomorrow's worries.
- We feel that if we could just get ourselves organized, we might be able to get everything done.

Which of the above telltale signs are most prevalent in your life currently?

_____

_____

_____

Carving Out a Space for Grace

In his follow-up book, *Sanctuary*, Hershey explains that we need to carve out "space for grace"—places and times that we call "sanctuary"—because such times and places renew, replenish, and nourish us. So, how do we go about doing that? Here are some suggestions.

- *Observe a weekly Sabbath day of rest.* In addition to having a day off from work, be sure to use this day for spiritual enrichment. For Catholics, participating in the celebration of the Eucharist is the central act in keeping the day holy. In addition to this, strive to unplug from various devices as much as possible and go "off the grid" to avoid distractions and stresses. Enjoy recreation—alone or with others—and rest, including taking a nap (as Elijah did!). This day should then serve as a prototype of the spirituality we carry with us the rest of the week: a spirituality characterized by patterns of prayer, reflection, and faith-sharing.

- *Build "Sabbath moments" into your daily routine.* Designate a time and place for practicing about ten minutes of stillness daily, in solitude if possible. Use this time to still your mind and to be physically still in your "sanctuary," enjoying your "inner chapel," to borrow a phrase from author, speaker, and spiritual director Becky Eldredge and her book *The Inner Chapel*.

- Practice some deep breathing to assist your transition into stillness.

- *Incorporate some extended Sabbath time into your yearly calendar.* In addition to going on vacation (which can often be just as stressful as work time), be sure to plan some time (a day or a few days) for an extended "Sabbath experience" or "personal retreat," so that you can regain your perspective and renew your disposition. Spend some time outdoors in nature if possible so that you can get in touch with the "white space" in your soul—that space

where God is more easily recognized. Do this several times a
year, if possible, perhaps to mark the change of seasons or other
transitions in your life.

In her book *Spiritual Practices for the Brain*, Anne Kertz Kernion
reminds us that it was St. John of the Cross who recommended that
we "carve out a day every week, or an hour a day, or a moment each
hour, and abide in the loving silence of the Friend." To remain vigilant
in this task, it can help to subscribe to a service such as the *3-Minute
Retreat* from Loyola Press, which invites you to take a short prayer
break right at your computer or on your phone, spending some quiet
time reflecting on a brief Scripture passage (www.loyolapress.com/
3-minute-retreats-daily-online-prayer).

When, where, and how do you experience "sanctuary"?

_____

_____

_____

The Benefits of Being Still

On a spiritual level, taking time to be still increases our awareness of
the following:

- *It reminds us that God is in charge.* Being busy all the time and
  spending all our time "doing" can be very deceptive. It makes us
  feel as though we are in control. Engaging in stillness reminds
  us that we are not in charge of our own destiny. Rather, we

cooperate with God, who is truly in charge. This realization is liberating because it takes pressure off us.

- *It reminds us that we can truly KNOW God.* To enter or deepen any relationship, we need to literally stop and engage the other person, listening to them and sharing with them. In the same way, when we take time to be still, we can more readily speak to God and listen to God speaking to our hearts. Stillness helps us move beyond thinking of God simply as a concept and instead move into a deeper relationship with the Divine.

- *It generates gratitude.* When we are still—and especially when we enjoy that stillness in nature—we come to a greater awareness of God's goodness. And the natural response to being the beneficiary of such goodness is gratitude, a disposition that brings us into contact with divine energy.

- *It reminds us that God is near to us.* Too often, we imagine God as distant, standing apart from our real life and daily affairs. When we enter stillness, we are better able to recognize and even feel the nearness of God. Scripture reminds us that God's presence is revealed in many ways and not usually with trumpet blasts or thunder and lightning. The story of Elijah seeking God's presence (1 Kings 19:11–13) tells us that God was not in the dramatic fires, earthquakes, and mighty winds but in a tiny whispering sound. Unless we are still, we will miss the whisper of God.

- *It humbles us.* It's humbling to appear in silence before someone. Our tendency is to speak our minds and let our opinions and feelings be known to all. To button our lips is to humble ourselves and open up to the thoughts of another, in this case, the thoughts of the Creator of the universe. By virtue of our humbling stillness, we encounter the Divine and are fortified by divine strength and energy.

Which of the above benefits are you most in need of experiencing in your life?

_____

_____

_____

Let Your Brain "Lie Fallow"

In agriculture, farmers are known to allow a field to "lie fallow" or unseeded for a season. This allows the soil to regain nutrients and become more fertile again instead of becoming further depleted. By allowing a field to lie fallow, the farmer assists in the field's renewal.

The stillness that we have been addressing in this chapter can be thought of along the same lines. We need to allow our brains to lie fallow so that they can be renewed, recharged, and replenished. A well-rested mind will be more fertile and will produce more fruit in the long run. Sometimes we simply need to do NOTHING! This is countercultural in a society that encourages almost obsessive activity and productivity. Fortunately, scientific research is revealing that downtime is not only underappreciated but is also a prerequisite to many complex cognitive processes.

When was a time you allowed your brain to "lie fallow" and, as a result, felt renewed and refreshed?

_____

_____

_____

To Grow Spiritually, Follow the Science

In *Spiritual Practices for the Brain*, Anne Kertz Kernion shares the following:

> It's not surprising that ancient wisdom about breath and being present is confirmed in today's science and discovery. Psychologists Matthew Killingsworth and Daniel Gilbert conducted a huge study with more than fifteen thousand people and 650,000 data points, concluding that almost half the time, subjects were not paying attention to the present moment. Their attention was on the future or on reprocessing a past event. When we live like this, we aren't happy, because our minds aren't here, now. Their main conclusion is that we must ground ourselves in the present moment to nurture happiness.

To be grounded in the present moment, and thus, to nurture happiness, it helps us to pause occasionally and be still—to BE in the moment. Research shows that for the brain to be productive and creative, it requires unstructured downtime. Such downtime is not to be confused with "vegging out" in front of the TV or immersing ourselves in video games or social media apps, all of which still require focused attention.

In an article published in *NeuroLeadership Journal* ("The Healthy Mind Platter"), researchers asserted that creativity relies on a number of cognitive processes, some of which are unconscious. These unconscious processes, including our imagination, occur only when we are not focused on a specific task. That is, they occur during downtime. This kind of downtime can be characterized as inactivity when we have no specific goal or focus in mind or, as the authors of the article say, "intentionally having no intention." Their research is showing that what once was dismissed as wasting time is now known to be a necessary ingredient of creative insight and complex decision making. It's no surprise that the third commandment about Sabbath rest is backed up by science!

When was the last time you truly experienced some downtime (not just "vegging out"), and what made that experience productive?

_____

_____

_____

Stillness Is Not Necessarily a State of Zen

When we talk about experiencing stillness, we are not necessarily talking about seeking a state of Zen—in Buddhist tradition, a state of mind that is achieved through meditation as one seeks enlightenment. This is indeed a worthy practice. However, you do not have to have formal periods of meditation to experience stillness. The kind of stillness we are talking about in this chapter is simply a slowing down; a quieting down, to shift one's consciousness and deepen one's awareness of the Divine, whose energy, like a river, is flowing just beneath the surface for us to tap into.

Such stillness can be achieved in just a few short moments by turning attention to one's breathing. One of the simplest methods for focusing on your breathing is called the 4-7-8 method, which follows these steps.

1. Begin by exhaling completely through your mouth, emptying your lungs, and feeling your diaphragm relax.
2. Close your mouth and breath in slowly through your nose as you count to four.
3. Hold your breath as you count to seven.
4. Slowly exhale through your mouth as you count to eight.
5. Repeat this cycle three more times.

This method is guaranteed to bring about some degree of relaxation and calm while reducing stress. You can practice this method while driving, at work, before undertaking an important task, during a stressful moment, before you go to sleep, when you wake up, as a first step in your prayer or meditation, and so on. You might consider saying or calling to mind the phrase "Be still and know that I am God" as you slowly inhale, as a way of turning the exercise into a more prayerful moment.

Practice the 4-7-8 breathing exercise. Describe how you feel afterward.

_____

_____

A Remedy for Restlessness

Stillness and calmness are the antitheses of restlessness. St. Augustine famously said, "Our hearts are restless, Lord, until they find rest in you." We humans do tend to be a restless lot. Adam and Eve, our first parents, were so restless that they couldn't sit still and enjoy the shade of the Tree of Knowledge of Good and Evil, but instead they were compelled to get up and pick its fruit. We have inherited this spiritual restlessness that causes us to resist being content in God's arms and drives us to seek fulfillment in all the wrong places rather than in the Divine.

Restlessness is also an impediment to intimacy. Think about it. If you were attempting to create a romantic moment with a significant other but couldn't get him or her to sit still, you would eventually give up in frustration. Lovers tend to look into one another's eyes, which is difficult to do if one partner can't be still. Stillness enables us to look into the eyes of God and God to gaze into our eyes. In fact, the word *reconciliation* includes the Latin word *cilia* (eyelashes), which means that to be reconciled with God is to come face-to-face with God, for our eyelashes to comingle with God's

In what area(s) of your life are you experiencing restlessness right now? When was a time that you felt "eyelash to eyelash" with God and that your relationship with God was intimate? What can you do to "reconcile" your relationship with God?

_____

_____

_____

Go Sleep!

I'm always impressed by the number of things that young parents teach their children: how to walk, talk, go potty, drink from a cup, share their toys, say please and thank you, tie their shoes, look both ways before crossing the street, and so on. Of course, one of the most crucial things that parents teach their children—not only for the child's sake but also for their own sake and sanity—is how to sleep! Sleep is absolutely critical for one's good health in mind, body, and spirit.

When I was a child, one of my dad's favorite lines to us children at nighttime (there were nine of us!) was "Go Sleep!" He would playfully growl in a deep voice: "Goooooo Sleeeeeep!" And while he did it playfully, we knew that he meant business! Good thing, too, because lack of sleep can have serious consequences, not only physically but also emotionally and spiritually.

It is common for people to feel different at nighttime than they do during the day. The darkness can increase fear and anxiety and make us feel more emotionally and spiritually vulnerable. We become more aware of thoughts and feelings as well as bumps in the night. Throughout Scripture we find references to light and darkness, day and night, including references to people having difficulty falling asleep.

- This was my situation: The heat consumed me in the daytime and the cold at night, and sleep fled from my eyes. (Genesis 31:40)

- When I lie down, I think, "How long before I get up?" The night drags on, and I toss till dawn. (Job 7:4)

- Night pierces my bones; my gnawing pains never rest. (Job 30:17)

- My heart falters, fear makes me tremble; the twilight I longed for has become a horror to me. (Isaiah 21:4)
- You said, "Woe to me! The LORD has added sorrow to my pain; I am worn out with groaning and find no rest." (Jeremiah 45:3)
- Then the king returned to his palace and spent the night without eating and without any entertainment being brought to him. And he could not sleep. (Daniel 6:18)
- While Pilate was sitting on the judge's seat, his wife sent him this message: "Don't have anything to do with that innocent man, for I have suffered a great deal today in a dream because of him." (Matthew 27:19)
- I have labored and toiled and have often gone without sleep; I have known hunger and thirst and have often gone without food; I have been cold and naked. (2 Corinthians 11:27)

In referring to sleeplessness, the Bible is not trying to raise awareness about sleep disorders any more than it is trying to raise awareness of vision or hearing impairments by telling stories of Jesus curing people who are blind or deaf. All of these have spiritual meanings. In Scripture, the inability to sleep is indicative of spiritual woes. In the same way, restful sleep is indicative of spiritual contentment.

- I lie down and sleep; I wake again, because the LORD sustains me. (Psalm 3:5)
- I will lie down and sleep in peace, for you alone, O LORD, make me dwell in safety. (Psalm 4:8)
- You will not fear the terror of night, nor the arrow that flies by day. (Psalm 91:5)
- Be at rest once more, O my soul, for the LORD has been good to you. (Psalm 116:7)

- When you lie down, you will not be afraid; when you lie down, your sleep will be sweet. (Proverbs 3:24)

Suffice it to say that if you want to tap into divine energy, get a good night's sleep. It is a deeply spiritual act!

> **How would you characterize your sleeping habits? What can you do to improve your sleeping habits?**
>
> _____
>
> _____
>
> _____

Inspiration from an Unlikely Source: The Three Stooges

My final thought for this section on sleep is inspired by an unlikely source: Moe Howard of the Three Stooges. Moe was famously perturbed by the shenanigans of his fellow stooges, especially the antics of his brothers, Curly and Shemp. One of Moe's pet peeves was being kept up at night by the noisy snoring of Curly or Shemp. To address the situation, Moe would rouse the noisy snorer and exclaim, "Wake up and go to sleep!"

For our purposes, we will put a slightly different spin on that phrase made famous by Moe. Instead of "Wake up and go to sleep!" my exhortation is for you to "Go to sleep and wake up!" In other words, if we hope to "get up" and tap into divine energy, we need to get our rest. Even Elijah was allowed to press the snooze button and sleep a while longer before the angel roused him a second time! An important part of our "being still" is a healthy sleep pattern.

GOOOOO SLEEEEEEP!

How much sleep are you getting each night on the average? How does lack of sleep affect you? What can you do to ensure more quality sleep?

_____

_____

_____

Stillness and Gratitude

One of the benefits of stillness is that it generates gratitude as our awareness of God's goodness grows. I have found, throughout my life, that the most effective first step in shaking off spiritual cobwebs and rising out of a spiritual rut is to give thanks. Gratitude assists us in emerging from the vicious circle of depression and into the virtuous circle of grace.

I'm sure you have found yourself caught in a vicious circle before. For example, you find yourself feeling a little down, so you treat yourself to a snack, a drink, or a purchase—only to find that the extra weight you've gained, the trouble you've gotten into with excessive drinking, or the piling debt you're being buried under leads you to feeling a little down—and to make yourself feel better, you repeat the behavior, and the cycle continues! Well, there's a different kind of circle we can and should get caught in: a virtuous circle! This occurs when we pause in stillness to reflect on all that we are grateful for, which leads to an attitude of gratitude and ultimately to a desire to serve others generously. Then, when we reflect on that experience with gratefulness, the cycle continues. This is why St. Paul encouraged disciples of Jesus to give thanks in all things (1 Thessalonians 5:18).

> **When was a time you found yourself languishing in a vicious circle as described above? What helped you emerge from this experience?**
>
> _____
>
> _____
>
> _____

Gratitude Is Good for You

Until recent times, the study of gratitude has been primarily relegated to the fields of philosophy and theology. In recent decades, however, psychology has emphasized the study of positive realities such as gratitude, happiness, hope, forgiveness, and compassion. While theology has long seen gratitude as a virtue, recent psychological studies have revealed that gratitude also has positive mental, physical, and emotional effects, one of which is heightened energy levels. Giving thanks—expressing gratitude—is indeed one of the most powerful ways for us to "get up" and tap into divine energy.

Having an attitude of gratitude is not to be equated with being oblivious to pain and suffering. The beauty of gratitude is that it is capable of existing alongside negative realities and, indeed, can help us navigate such storms. We become especially fortified against such negativity when gratitude grows beyond an occasional (and fleeting) emotion and into a permanent trait—a disposition.

So, whenever your angel comes along and urges you to "get up" out of whatever spiritual malaise you may be experiencing, I recommend you respond by pausing in stillness and then making a list of what you are thankful for. By doing so, you will enable gratitude to permeate all the suggestions I've offered in this book to tap into divine energy: create something, delight in nature, simplify your life, celebrate relationships, show compassion, make repairs, share generously and selflessly, and be still.

So, let me conclude this final chapter by saying, thank you! Now . . . GET UP!

> **Take a moment to quiet yourself and then compile a list of things (big or small) that you are thankful for. Come back to this list frequently and add to it so that it is always growing.**
>
> _____
>
> _____
>
> _____

In Summary . . .

God knows that we need to rest and even "commands" that we do so once per week (the Sabbath). All the world's great spiritual traditions have deemed it necessary to "be still" to connect with the Divine.

We are called to build Sabbath time into our daily routine (at least a few moments), our weekly schedule (at least one day), and throughout the year (extended periods of rest). It is in resting that we realign ourselves with God and renew ourselves so that we can become more fully human and tap into divine energy.

Scripture Passages That Reveal/Emphasize God's Call for Us to Be Still

Be still before the LORD and wait patiently for him.
Psalm 37:7

Be still, and know that I am God.
Psalm 46:10

My soul finds rest in God alone;
  my salvation comes from him.
Psalm 62:1

But I have stilled and quieted my soul;
  like a weaned child with its mother,
  like a weaned child is my soul within me.
Psalm 131:2

In repentance and rest is your salvation,
  in quietness and trust is your strength.
Isaiah 30:15

Then, because so many people were coming and going that they did not even have a chance to eat, he said to them, "Come with me by yourselves to a quiet place and get some rest."
Mark 6:31

Which of the above Scripture quotes speaks to you most strongly about the spiritual benefits of being still? Why?

_____

_____

_____

As you reflect on this chapter, what is one shift you can make in your life to tap into the divine energy of stillness?

_____

_____

_____

Conclusion:
The Time Has Come

Regain your senses, call yourself back, and once again wake up.
—Marcus Aurelius

A Wake-Up Call

Most wake-up calls are not pleasant.

I'm not talking about the kind of wake-up call you get by telephone when staying in a hotel so that you don't miss your morning meeting. I'm talking about the kind of wake-up call associated with having a heart attack, getting pulled over for a DUI, losing a job you thought you'd have forever, losing a loved one, experiencing a financial loss, or having a close relative or friend attempt suicide.

Such wake-up calls are a kick in the gut that compels us to pause and reflect on our life and consider making some significant changes in our perspective, our behavior, or our attitude. The good news, however, is that we don't have to experience something painful to have a wake-up call. At any point in our life, we can pause, take stock, review and evaluate, and make changes. It's called repentance, and it is the call that Jesus led with when he proclaimed the Good News: "The time has come," he said. "The kingdom of God is near. Repent and believe the good news!" (Mark 1:15).

Change Your Mind

Repentance is not to be confused with being sorry for a laundry list of sins. Repentance is the changing of one's mind, one's perspective, one's behavior, or one's attitude in order to "live again." It is what the angel called Elijah to. It is a call to come forth from the tomb, just as Jesus called forth Lazarus, so that we might awaken from "dead-ness" and experience new life. It is a turning point. The heart of the gospel of Jesus Christ is an invitation to experience a turning point—an opportunity to let go of our exhausting efforts to be self-sufficient and to instead tap into divine energy and a renewed life: this is the foundation of authentic discipleship.

You will face turning points in your life and, unfortunately, many of them will be precipitated by painful events such as the ones mentioned above. This need not be. The Holy Spirit makes the transformative grace of God available at any moment in life to help us change our priorities, our perspectives, our attitudes, and our behaviors. Why wait? The time has come.

Consider this your wake-up call!

"Wake up, O sleeper, rise from the dead, and Christ will shine on you" (Ephesians 5:14).

Bibliography

Buchanan, Kathryn and Anat Bardi. "Acts of Kindness and Acts of Novelty Affect Life Satisfaction." *The Journal of Social Psychology* 150 (2010): 235–37.

Corwin, Anna I. *Embracing Age: How Catholic Nuns Became Models of Aging Well*. New Brunswick, NJ: Rutgers University Press, 2021.

Covey, Stephen R. *The 7 Habits of Highly Effective People: Powerful Lessons in Personal Change*. New York: Simon & Schuster, 2004.

Dunn, Elizabeth, Lara Aknin, and Michael Norton. "Spending Money on Others Promotes Happiness." *Science* 319 (2008): 1687–88.

Eldredge, Becky. *The Inner Chapel: Embracing the Promises of God*. Chicago: Loyola Press, 2020.

Hershey, Terry. *The Power of Pause: Becoming More by Doing Less*. Chicago: Loyola Press, 2011.

———. *Sanctuary: Creating a Space for Grace*. Chicago: Loyola Press, 2015.

Ignatius of Loyola, Saint. *The Spiritual Exercises of St. Ignatius Loyola: A New Translation*. Translated by Elisabeth Meier Tetlow. Lanham, MD: University Press of America, 1987.

Kernion, Anne Kertz. *Spiritual Practices for the Brain: Caring for Mind, Body, and Soul.* Chicago: Loyola Press, 2020.

Konrath, Sara, Andrea Fuhrel-Forbis, Alina Lou, and Stephanie Brown. "Motives for Volunteering Are Associated with Mortality Risk in Older Adults." *Health Psychology:* 31 (2011): 87–96.

Nouwen, Henri J. M. *With Open Hands.* Notre Dame, IN: Ave Maria Press, 1972.

Poelmans, Steven, David Rock, Daniel Siegel, and Jessica Payne. "The Healthy Mind Platter." *NeuroLeadership Journal* 4 (2012): 1–23.

Pope Francis. *Laudato Si': On Care for Our Common Home.* Vatican City: Vatican Publishing House, 2015.

Pope John Paul II. *Letter to Artists.* Vatican City: Vatican Publishing House, 1999.

Price, Catherine. *The Power of Fun: How to Feel Alive Again.* New York: The Dial Press, 2021.

Ree, Amanda. "7 Spiritual Lessons from Your Pet." Chopra.com, 17 Sept. 2020.

Roman Missal. Washington, D.C: Office of Public Services, United States Catholic Conference, 1982.

Thibodeaux, Mark E. *Reimagining the Ignatian Examen: Fresh Ways to Pray from Your Day.* Chicago: Loyola Press, 2015.

Vogt, Susan. *Blessed by Less: Clearing Your Life of Clutter by Living Lightly.* Chicago: Loyola Press, 2013.

Wright, N. T. *Simply Christian: Why Christianity Makes Sense.* San Francisco: HarperSanFrancisco, 2006.

About the Author

Joe Paprocki, DMin, has served as National Consultant for Faith Formation at Loyola Press since 2002. Joe, who has over 40 years of experience in pastoral ministry, has authored over twenty books on catechesis and pastoral ministry and has presented in over 150 dioceses in North America. Joe received his Masters of Pastoral Studies from the Institute of Pastoral Studies/Loyola University of Chicago and his Doctor of Ministry from the University of St. Mary of the Lake/Mundelein Seminary. He blogs about his catechetical experiences and insights at www.catechistsjourney.com. Joe and his wife Joanne live just outside of Chicago where they now enjoy life as grandparents.

Also by Joe Paprocki

7 KEYS TO SPIRITUAL WELLNESS

Enriching Your Faith by Strengthening the Health of Your Soul

In *7 Keys to Spiritual Wellness*, best-selling author Joe Paprocki provides a prescription for spiritual health based on the rich wisdom of Catholic Tradition. Through his nondogmatic, downright inviting style of writing, Paprocki makes this book accessible to non-Catholics and "seekers" as well.

Recognizing that the spiritual immune system is weakened almost daily by toxic patterns and attitudes that negatively impact our ability to live in a harmonious relationship with God and others, Paprocki offers seven enduring and reliable strategies for achieving spiritual wellness, along with seven persistent dangers to our spiritual well-being that can manifest themselves in our lives.

At its core, *7 Keys to Spiritual Wellness* helps us see the Christian faith not as a collection of rules and doctrine, but as a spiritual path—a path whose guideposts for spiritual wellness are sure to lead us to a more meaningful life and to a much richer experience of our faith.

LOYOLAPRESS.
A JESUIT MINISTRY

Find it at **store.loyolapress.com** or wherever books are sold.

Also by Joe Paprocki

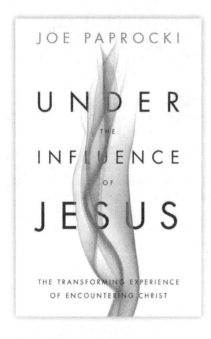

UNDER THE INFLUENCE OF JESUS

The Transforming Experience of Encountering Christ

It was during the feast of Pentecost when a dejected, cowering, frightened group of Jesus' closest followers were suddenly transformed by the Holy Spirit into exceptionally bold proclaimers of a life-changing message. But what was the message they were proclaiming? Moreover, is it really possible that a very specific proclamation from nearly 2,000 years ago can actually transform people today?

In *Under the Influence of Jesus,* best-selling author Joe Paprocki offers an emphatic answer to that question: Yes, it can! Throughout the book, Paprocki explores not only the various elements of the message itself—such as the kingdom of God, the cross, the Resurrection, sin, and conversion—but also the particular characteristics of a changed heart and life that result from accepting the message that Jesus is Lord and that we are now a "new creation" in a new kind of kingdom.

Candidly and accessibly written, *Under the Influence of Jesus* is ultimately an invitation to encounter Christ in a whole new way, to thrive under his lordship, and to use our own transformed hearts and lives to help bring others into a life-changing relationship with Jesus.